I Din't Say Nothin' . . . ag'in!

Michael Brindid

Published by M Brindid
Orfanon
The Green
Hickling
Norwich
Norfolk NR12 0XR

ISBN 0 9529832 5 9

Also by Michael Brindid
I Dint' Say Nothin'!

Cover photograph curtesy
The Eastern Daily Press

Produced by Jim Baldwin
Fakenham, Norfolk

Printed in England

A Product of Fakenham

Introduction

The letters that emanate every month from Orfanon at Hickling, so vital a part of the correspondence to the Eastern Daily Press for many years, are a glorious marriage of warm dialect and soft Norfolk humour. What began as a letter to the editor has gently grown beyond measure, such has been Michael Brindid's popular success recording his prose for posterity.

It comes as no surprise whatsoever that what he would call his modest efforts to uphold Norfolk's dialect have blossomed into two books and a readership far beyond his beloved county's border. I know this volume, like the first, will give enormous pleasure to the many people who cherish local character and colour and who value the efforts of people like Michael who strive to sustain it. He is to be congratulated for achieving so much, and achieving it in such a delightful, understated and genuine way.

May the pen never dry Michael!

Martin Kirby
Deputy Editor
Eastern Daily Press

Foreword

It is true to say I have known Michael all my life, since one of my earliest recollections as a child is of him living almost next door. We have our roots in the same part of Norfolk and were both exposed to the same rich vein of bucolic characters who formed the backdrop to our daily lives. We grew up with similar strict non conformist influences shaping our future. For all of his working life he plied his trade as a carpenter in and around the locality, always listening and learning about the people, their ways and their peculiar idiosyncrasies.

Michael has always taken a genuine interest in local people, absorbing yarns and apocryphal tales recounted over years, by rustic raconteurs. You have to live and be brought up here to genuinely understand and appreciate the unique blend of humour and logic that makes up the Norfolk character. The indigenous Norfolkman is never awkward or unwelcoming but he does like to "do different". It is from this kind of background that Michael Brindid's understanding of the Norfolk dialect grew.

Michael's interesting and humorous accounts which regularly regale the letters section in the Eastern Daily Press are strictly original but the medium for delivering it, the Norfolk dialect, goes back over many generations reflecting, in his case a lifetime of vigilant observation.

I count it a privilege to be invited to write the forward to "I Din't Say Nothin' Ag'in", Michael's second book and feel sure that all who read it will thoroughly enjoy it.

David Osborne

(David Osborne is Headteacher of Wroughton Middle School in Gorleston)

The Artist

Bridget Parsons produces all the delightful illustrations used in my books and I know that readers will agree that she does a splendid job.

Born in Maidstone, Kent, Bridget obtained a GCSE in Art and was a scenery painter for the Maidstone Players but did not take up art as a profession. Instead she moved to London to train as a nurse at The London Hospital and it was while she was there that she met and married John, later moving to Essex.

Bridget found Norfolk 25 years ago when she took on the renovation of a 370 year old derelict flint cottage next to Hickling Staithe. She took up illustrating shortly after arriving in Hickling, doing designs for tea towels, sweatshirts etc for village church fund raising. In addition to this Bridget paints and exhibits locally, her speciality being painting on glass.

With three daughters and five grandchildren and a job as a classroom assistant at Hickling School I am more than pleased that she has found the time to draw pictures of me and the missus.

Michael Brindid

The Missus

Norah Brindid originated from a humble but happy Methodist farm labourers home at East Ruston, where she attended the village Primary School until eleven years of age when she passed the Eleven Plus Scholarship to the North Walsham Girls High School and went there up to the age of sixteen.

She was a GPO Telephonist all her single working life - forty one and a half years at Norwich and four and a half at Great Yarmouth, during this time relieving at Eastbourne, North Walsham, Sheringham and Brundall.

She married Michael in 1952. Both are Methodists with a common love of music which brought them together and still continues through their daughter Carol and grandaughters Lucy and Rebekah.

After her marriage Norah worked as Welfare Assistant at the Hickling Primary School. Since her retirement she still goes voluntarily to play for Assembly.

Much of her time is now given to supporting Michael's interest in the Norfolk Dialect.

Michael Brindid

Acknowledgements

J ust being there - helping me with my mail, typing, recording, and showing an interest in what started off as a hobby, yet grown to a point that I could not have envisaged way back in 1991. Supporting me throughout has been my wife Norah - (The Missus) and I pay tribute to her and dedicate "I Din't Say Nothin' Ag'in" to her, my family and Norfolk people wherever they may be.

To the Eastern Daily Press and their staff I say "well done" and thank them for publishing a hundred letters written in Norfolk dialect all reminding people that Norfolk is a very special place.

Martin Kirby, a Norfolk man, and Deputy Editor at the Eastern Daily Press, and himself a writer enjoys playing his part in helping Norfolk retain its character. He shows a personal interest in my writing. I thank him for readily agreeing to write the forward to my second book "I Din't Say Nothin' Ag'in"

David Osborne, now living on the borders of Hickling has been in the teaching profession all his working life. He writes Norfolk Dialect Songs and enjoys entertaining locally. Both David and I are members of the Hickling Methodist Church where he plays a major role. He is now Headteacher of Wroughton Middle School in Gorleston and feels proud to be asked to contribute to "I Din't Say Nothin' Ag'in".

Bridget Parson's illustrations for my first book were much appreciated and enjoyed by many. For this reason I was happy to ask her for a repeat performance. The result can be seen and will, I am sure, bring a smile to readers faces.

My thanks to Jim Baldwin for producing "I Din't Say Nothin' Ag'in" in such a professional way, which only he is capable of.

Micael Brindid
Hickling
April 1998

In the ind, the plearce wus in an uproar...

March, 1995

I wus a-listenin' ter the City's match on the ole wireless a Saturda arternoon.

The missus wus hevin' har annual bath. She shouted: "Are we a-gorn' out ternite?" I say, "If yer want tew." "What dew yer think I oter wear?" she say. I say, "Yew'll hatter put more on than yer got on now tha's fer sure." She spent the next hour a-trickolairtin' harself up. She say ter me, "Aren't yew a-comin' yit, tha's gittin' dark alriddy."

So we went round the cust ter Bacton. Wen we got there she reckoned she fancied a small harf. We stopped at a nice plearce and sat at a tearble near a winda tha' looked out ter sea. Not tha' we could see a lot corse tha' wus as black as the hairkes. She hed wot she wanted an' let me hev a glass o' wine, but unly one on account o' me a-drivin'. (Sumtimes I think tha' ud be nice if she could dew the drivin'!)

We stayed an' hed a little mardle then got in the car ter cum humm. She say, "Dorn't go yit, I're left my gloves. I'll go back an' git 'em. Yew cum wi' me." Wen we got ter the tearble where we'd bin a-sittin' sum more fooks sat there. The missus say, "I're lorst my gloves, hev yew sin 'em?" They got up an' hed a look. The people at the next tearble did the searme. Afore long the plearce wus in an uproar with evryone a-lookin' fer har gloves. In the ind, the blook wot own the plearce cum uver. He say, "Wus a-gorn on here?" The missus say, "I're lorst my gloves." He say, "Leave it ter me, I'll git my clearners ter hev a look in the mornin' an' I'll give yew a ring if they find 'em."

She thort he wus ever ser nice.

On the way humm we stopped at Stallum fer fish an' chips. Tha' put har in a good mind. When we got humm she took har coat an' har little lambs wool hat orf. Yew're not gorn' ter berlieve this but har gloves warr in the top o' har hat, so all the while we warr a-lookin' for 'em she was a-wearin' 'em on top o' har hid. Did yew ever know anyone ser sorft!

"I've lorst mer gloves."

At the moment I'm in
har good books

April, 1995

Tha's a rummin' how yer cen git involved inter suffin' yer din't bargain for.

The missus nipped up the shop tuther mornin'. As she wus a-comin out, she saw a woman she hent seen fer a long time. The missus say, "Hello, how a yew a-gitten on?" "Not very well," she say, "I fair rotten." The missus say, "Cum ter think on it, yew dorn't look too good. Yew din't orter be out in this cold wind." The woman say, "I cum ter git a tin o' soup. Tha's all I fancy." The missus say, "Yew go humm, I'll go an' git my ole bike an' cum an' see yer."

Where this woman live, tha's everso lonela. When she got there, the missus nearla hed a fit. The washin' up han't bin done fer dairs, an' she set hid an' knees in front o' the fire in the front room wi' her cutt on. The missus say, "I'll put a hot wa'er bo'le in yar bed. Yew go an' put yar hid down an' I'll bring yew a cup o' corfee, then when I git humm I'll ring the doctor an' arsk him ter cum out an' see yer."

She say ter the missus, "Will yer cum back agin lairter?"
We hed our tea an' the missus say, "Will yer tearke me up there?" I say, "I'd rather keep here near the fire." She say, "Dorn't yew know wot tha' say in the Bible?" I say, "Yis, tha' say arter a man a bin ter wark all day he're go' ter put his feet up an' keep warm." "Cum on," she say, "Tha' ent gorn' ter tearke long in the motor, an' I'll do the washin' up wen we git back instead o' yew." Then she gav me the story about the Good Samaritan. In the ind I thort tha' wus fair enuff, so I took 'er.

Wen we got there, the missus say, "Did the doctor cum?" She say, "Yis, he hed ter see my nearba, so he said he'd kill two badds wi' one stunn." (Arterwards, the missus reckon tha' warn't a wery nice thing fer him ter say.) He told har ter keep in bed fer a dair an' tearke sum pills he left forr'er. There wus I, a-pruggin' about in the dark, choppin' kinlin' an' cartin' in coal an' helpin' the missus ter do this blummin' washin' up. Tha' wus little arter ten o'clock afor we got humm. Arter all said an' done, tha' wus nice ter think we war airble ter help, an' the missus told me she wus ever ser grairtful, so at the moment I'm in har good books but I dorn't know how long for.

'You din't orter be out in this cold wind.'

The washing wurra nice shearde o' green...

May, 1995

I go' suffen wrong agin larst Munda mornin'. Tha's a pity corse I was unla tryin' ter help.

Tha's like this 'ere. We're hed our mawther Carol an' har two gals here fer nigh on a week. They warra packin' up riddy ter go in the arternoon. The missus told Carol she'd do har washin' afor she went so she din't hev it ter do wen she got humm.

I said: "I'll do the washin'." The missus say: "Oh yew are kind." (Or wadds ter tha' effect.) I wus the blue-eyed boy fer a time, but tha' feelin' warn't gorn' ter last fer long.

We hen't go' a washin' machine, just a boiler an' a spinner. I filled the copper wi' sorft water from our butt, hulled all this datty washin' in, put in the Persil an wairted forrit ter boil. Arter they'd boiled, I took the washin' out wi' the missus's copper stick, an' give 'em a good rinse in the sink. Yew never see ser much stuff. Yew tearke smalls from fowr femearles, tha's anuff ter fill a barra. Enyhow I put 'em in the spinner an thort: "This is easy, I can't think why the missus mearke ser much fuss about a bit o' washin'." Then she cum in ter see how I wus a-gittin' on. Well, bor did she carry on!

I doesn't tell yer wot she called me. Yer see, evrything wus the searme colour. There wus sheets, towels etc, an' all these smalls wurra nice shearde o' green. I'd put a green skat o' the missus in an' boiled the lot tergather.

When she quietened down a bit she say: "A child o' five would a-known batter. Why din't yer read the learbles?" The Carol hed a go at me an' the kids joined in, so I say: "There's nothin' I cen do now" an' said I wus sorry.

Ter mearke amends I'd go an' hang 'em out on the ole linen line. Tha' wus a-blowin' a gairle. I thort they'd soon git dry in all tha' wind. I hung the sheet out fast. While I wus a-hangin' the other things, tha' took off at about fotty mile an hour, blew the length o'
the garden, an' finished up in a black-thorn hidge. Wot followed is too pairnful ter print. Just ter say apart from the odd "Yis" or "No" the missus hen't had too much ter say lairtla. Since we're bin hevin' nice wather she is comin' round a bit. In fact she did say: "En't nice now we're got the house ter ourselves.

I'll tell yer suffen', I be I dorn't git asked ter do the washin' agin.

"Tha' blew the length a the gardin".

A bed all ter merself on a second honeymune

June, 1995

The missus say, "Can't we hev a few nites away somewhere - sort uva second honeymune?"

I say, "Wot arter fotty tree years, dorn't talk ser sorft."

I thort the least said about tha' the batter. Then blow me, the next-er mornin' we hed a latter from a Hotel overlookin' the sea in Aldeburgh, tellin' us about sum mid-week brairks.

The missus say: "Tha' wus meant ter be. Shall we go?"

Ter keep the pearce I say, "Orite, book up if yer want to." She give this here plearce a ring, an' there wus one room left. Tha' wus number tharteen. Tha' put me orf fer a statt.

However, I needn't a-worried corse tha' wus a luvla hotel. There wus a big log fire a-bannin' in the lounge. We hed our own bathroom an' all tha' sort o' thing an' the food wus wery good.

The missus wus airble ter hev one a two small halves o' Adnams. Our bedroom wus very comfortable, but wairt forrit, - twin beds!

The missus say, "Tha's a bit ora blow ter kick orf with." In spite o' tha' we hed a good toime a-walkin round Minsmere, Dunwich and Orford an' afore yew could say "Norwich City", we were humm agin.

Tha's wen she statted. She say "I're hed nice toime but dew know the thing I injoyed the musst."

I say, "No, wot?" She say, "The twin beds. I'd fergot wot tha' wus loike ter hev a bed all ter merself. Tha's batter than hevin' yew a-snortin' an' snorin'. Why carn't we hev twin beds here?"

I din't say nothin' but I'd injoyed hevin' a bed ter myself too. I thort tha's no good me puttin' my foot down if I hen't got a leg ter stand on.

The next thing, she wus in the bedroom wi' har tearpmeasure. She say, "I we hull out the kids cot, pram an doll's house we'd hev enuff room. Tha'll mean yew'll hatter sleep up aginst the wall."

I say, "Wot about the bedside lamp? I carn't reach it." She say,
"I're thort o' tha'. Yew cen hev the torch an' keep on the floor so tha's handa if yew want a light in the night." I say, "Tha's a rummin' arter all these years we're gotta' cum ter this, the next thing yew'll want me ter move inter the spare room."

She say, "Not at the moment, le's give the twin beds a chance an' tearke each day as it cum."

If she git inter har hid she want suffen she's gorn ter hev it. Yew know wot she's like.

I thort she wus out o' one o' them horror fillums

July, 1995

I're writ fifta latters ter yew uver the last few year an' yit I'd never sin yer, so tha' was rite nice ter cum ter yar orffice an' shearke yer b'the hand.

Thanks fer givin' me the time ter hev a chat, an' see where tha' all happen.

I wus a-tellin' my missus about it wen I got humm. I say ter har, "Tha's a jolla good job yew din't go corse yew'd a got lorst in tha' gret ole plearce.

Torkin' about the missus, she git a bad hid now an' agin. She reckon tha's wen there's thunder about. If there's a tampest in North Wales har hid'll earke here in Norfolk.

So she got out an ole book called Natural Remedies for Common Ailments ter see wot tha' said about hidearkes. Tha' told yer ter put a slice o' cucumber on each eye an' tha' should git rid on it. She went ter bed an' wen I went inter the bedroom, there she lay wi' this here cucumber.

She put the breeze up me. She looked a job. I thort she wus someone out o' one o' them horror fillums. Enyhow, wen she wook up in the mornin' she reckon tha' was the cucumber wot done it. I din't say nothin'.

She say, "Hev yer got enything wrong wi' yew?" I say, "Not tha' I know on apart from a corn on one o' my toes." So she looked in the book under corns. She say, "Here y'ar I'll soon git rid o' tha'."

She went inter the backus an' cum back wirra crushed clove o' garlic. She say, "Tearke yer sock orf." I say, "Tenser likely." She say, "Tha' can't do ner harm if it dorn't do ner good."

I told har where this ole corn wus an' she tearped this garlic on mer toe.

She say, "Tha' say you're got ter leave it on fer two dairs. If yer leave it on longer tha'll tearke yer toe orf." She larft.

Well bor tha' wus a job wi' tha' ole garlic in bed. Torke about mearke yer eyes water, the plearce stunk o' garlic. I unla hoped tha' was gorn ter be wath it, but tha' wus just fer one nite, so tha' weren't too bad.

Artrer a couple o' dairs she say ter me, "How's yar corn?" I say, "I think tha's gittin' batta corse I can't feel nothin' on it." I took orf tha' there plaster, giv my foot a good soak, hed a pick here an' there, an' this bloomin' ole corn cum out as clean as a whistle.

So if yew it a corn, yew put some garlic on it, even if yew do git wrong orf yar missus. Tha'll stink the house out but tha'll do the job!

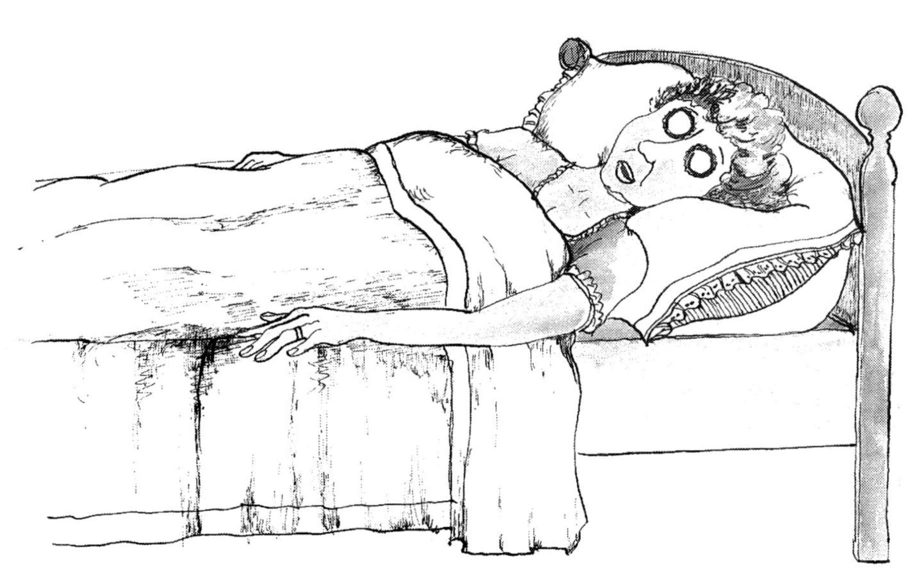

'She put the breeze up me.'

My missus, she's gorn away to look arter the grandorters...

August, 1995

I reckon you're bin a-wonderin' where I're bin a-gitten' to corse I hent writ ter yer leartly. Well, tha's like this, ever since yew advertised my book in yar pearper, my life a bin tanned upside down.

The pustman a bin bringin' ser many letters so I're hed me own elastic band round 'em. My missus reckon yew can't git higheran that. My book a bin sent ter Malaysia, USA, New Zealand, Scotland, an' just about evera county in England.

I pusted a lot on 'em ter Suffolk, sum even went ter Ipswich. My missus she say, "Do yer think yew orter send 'em there?" I say, " Why not?" She say, "Yew know Ipswich Town an' Norwich City. Things aren't too good at Norwich at the moment, the last thing they want is fer yew ter put the boot in."

She reckon I should ask Martin O'Neill wot he think. Did yer ever hear enyone tork ser much squit?

Enyhow she's gone away ter look arter the grandorters few a week a two. Ter statt orf with I thort tha' sounded like a good idea. I could do nothin' wen I wanted, or do nothin' at all. She left me plenty o' grub in. The fust day I thort I'd hev a lamb chop. I took two on 'em out o' the freezer. I onla wanted one but do yer think I could git them bloomin' things apart! I took 'em inter the shud an' split 'em open with a wood hook.

I'd got sum new tearters an' carrots I put this here chop in the oven (with a bit o' mint). All wus riddy - I'd just got ter weart forrit ter cook. Arter a while I hed a look in the ole oven an' tha' wus still cold. I'd put 'em in the top oven an' tanned the bottom one on. I hed ma dinner in the ind but tha' wus round about harf arter two.

From then on things went from bad ter wass. I wus given our spare bedroom a good ole muck out. I knew the missus ud be suffen pleased. I hulled out a lot o' ole boxes an' lumber, then I muvd the bed so I could give the floor a good ole do. I cam acrorse two spoons an' a harf a crown. I say ter myself, "Tha's a long time since she're

done under there. Then as I wus a-movin' stuff around I knocked uva the bedside lamp an' brook the sheard.

I thort, "She'll be suffin' savage so I tearped it tergather agin. I dorn't think she'll nutice unless someone gorn tell her.

Tha' mearke yer wonder wus gorn ter happen next. If yew do see the missus round Swaffum or Watton tell har ter hurry up an' cum hum. Yew carn't miss har. She'll be a-wearin' a white tea shat with a grat ole strawberry on the front with the wadds "Pick your own."

Red roses din't vev any effect on the missus

September, 1995

"Look at the steart o' tha' sink."

They war the fast wads the missus say wen she got humm arter bein' away fer a fortnite.

"How manna times hev I told you not ter empty the teapot in the sink?" she say. "Did yer git the vim?"

I say: "I think so."

She say: "I purrit on the list."

She looked in the cupboard an' there waren't no vim there. She say: "Yew din't git it did yer?" Wus the point o' hevin' a list if yew dorn't git wus on it?"

I say, "I'm sure I got it."

She cum acrors it learter on - I'd purrit in the food cupboard. Tha' wus a hind a box o' cornflearkes.

Yew orter-a-hard wot she said about tha'. I've gotta say her humm comin' din't wark out as I'd planned. I'd even put sum red roses in the bedroom. She did say "Thanks" but they din't hev any effect on her.

I just hoped cum the mornin' tha' she'd git back ter normal, but did she! - yew must be jokin! She sat about an' played har piana fer I dorn't know how long.

I say: "Aren't yew gorn ter do suffin?"

She say: "No I dorn't fair like it."

I say: "Wus wrong, dorn't yer fair well?"

She say: "Um orite, I've just got a bit o' jet lag."

"Strike a lite," I say, "Ye're onla bin ter Swaffum, not Canada."

Fer once she din't know wot ter say. Then she say, "I thort I told yew ter git yar hair cut while I wus away." I say, "I hen't had time."

She say, "I'd a thort you'd a mearde time. Wot must all o' them people think wot keep a ringin' yew up."

She just seem ter be lookin' fer any excuse ter hev a go at me an' she dorn't like it if I dorn't answer back.

Um a-wonderin' if the heat o' the last week a go anything anything ter do wirrut. She reckon she hin't got new go in har. She like it nice an warm but this larst few dears a bin a bit too much. The wather man reckon tha's gorn ter git cooler cum the weekend.

If tha's the hot wather wus a-gitten' har down, the sooner the weekend cum the batter. So if yew find yar missus a bit snappy, just keep calm an' hope we soon git a few frorsts.

" Are'nt yew gorn ter do suffin?"

Bit o' a ding dong tuther nite
with missus

October, 1995

The last time I wrut tew ya, I wus a-tellin' ya how unsettled the missus a bin since she cum humm arter bein' away fer a fortnite. I just can't mearke har out. Tha' mearke yer wonder wot she got up while she wus away. I dussn't say nothin' tew'er corse she'll onla bite my hid orf.

We hed a bit o' a ding dong tuther nite. I wus a-readin' the pearper wen I cum acrorse a pearge wirra hole in it, I say, "Wud yet cut the pearper for?" She say, "Tha's an advert." I say, "Wor for?" She say, "If I tell yer dorn't mob will yer." I say, "Try me."

She say, "Tha's frum a single man in his mid 40's who want lodgin's fer a few months in the Hicklin' area. He sound very nice. I wus a-thinkin' tha' ud be orite if we hed him here. He cen hev our spare room. Wudda yer think. Would yer like that?" I say, "I carn't think wus cum uva yer, corse I dorn't want him here."

She say, "Why dorn't yer look at it from my point o' view. Tha' mearke sense ter me, yew bein' out of an evenin' an' I'd enjoy the company - someone ter watch Coronairtion Street with. Yew could enjoy yerself all the more knowin' tha' I warn't on my own." I say, "Yew git yar way about must things, but I say we're not hevin' a lodger an ' tha's the ind on it."

Arter tha' she went all moody an' din't say a lot. Two or thre dairs lairter our mawther Carol rang ter say she could be on the muv agin an would we hev her cat. I say, "If a cat is gorn ter put this lodger out o' yer mind then yis, we'll hev the cat." The missus wus plearsed about tha', she say, "Even a cat cen be good compana."

So Carol brought the cat, an' she soon mearde harself at humm. The missus mearke sum fuss o' har. She let har sleep on the bed uv a daytime an' tha' git away wi' anythin. Yew should hear har tork to it. Wen the missus git up of a mornin' she go rite past me ter the cat an' say, "Hello my pet, hev yew hed a good nite. Yew are a good girl etc, etc."

I dorn't say nothin' corse the cat a got ter be batta then a lodger, but I carn't help a-thinkin', "Wen wus the larst time she spook ter me the way she tork ter tha' bloomin' cat."

"Hello my pet, hev yew hed a good nite?"

The missus dorn't hev a good nite

November, 1995

The heat o' the summer is uva, mearke no mistearke about tha'. The missus reckon she hen't bin too warm abed the larst nite a two, so she got out har eiderdowns. We're hed 'em 43 year, so yew can tell they dorn't look in the best o' health.

Wen she put 'em on the bed, she saw a hole a two wi' the fathers a-comin' out. She say: "These ole things a past the best. We orter git sum newuns."

She was a-tellin' our mawther Carol about it an' she say: "Wot yew wanta do Mum is ter git sum duvets. Yew an' Dad ud like them. They're nice an' cosy."

So the missus got two o' these things. The nearme o' the mearke on 'em is Cloud Nine.

The missus say: "I orfen think tha' must be nice ter be on Cloud Nine but there's no chance o' tha' a-livin' wi' yew, so I'll hev the next best thing an' be under Cloud Nine." She larft.

I say: "I dorn't think tha's wery funny." She say: "Sorry I din't mean it."

I must admit the bedroom look nice wi' buth beds lookin' the searme. The missus say: "I carn't weart ter cum ter bed ternite just ter try 'em out."

In the mornin' she say: "Did yer hev a good nite? Warr yer nice an' warm?" I say: "Yis, howd yew git on?" She say: "Not wery well. I wook up about tree. The bloomin' cover wus on the floor an' I wus nearly blue wi' cold so I go' a blanket an' put uva me." I say: "I go' on orite, I hed a good nite. The trouble wi' yew is yer dorn't lay still. Yew'll be orite once yew git the hang on 'em."

Enyhow, the nexta nite wus just the searme. Wen she wuk up she wus suffin' savige. She say: "Bloomin' things, I wish I'd never sin 'em. U'm gorn back ter how we warr." I say: "No yew arn't, we spent all tha' money on 'em an' ye're gorn ter stick it out."

She say: "Tha's orite fer yew, but if Um gorn ter be cold like tha' nite arter nite I'll git the flu or suffin'. I'll be batter orf a-sleepin' on the settee."

She'll hev a job ter do tha'. If yew warr ter see our settee of an evenin' yew'd know wot I mean. She sit in the middle. Buth sides on 'er is covered wi' wool, knittin' books, pins an' needles. Yew never see such a job. If yew warr ter sit enywhere near har, yew'd do yerself a mischif.

The phone rang tuther nite. She say: "Answer tha'." I say: "Where is it?" She'd hed it an' tha' wus under the cushions. She wus a-sittin' on it.

How much longer hev I got ter put up wi' this? Why carn't life be a bit more simple?

"Buth sides on 'er is covered
wi' wool, knitting books and pins etc."

New skatt or a fryin' pan: wot's best fer the missus?

December, 1995

I must say, if there's a time o' the year wen the missus is wath living with, tha's Christmas, so I'll try ter mearke the best on it while it larst. She say: "This year I aren't gorn ter to be caught nappin'. I'm gorn ter git ahid an' not leave evrathing ter the larst minute like I did larst year."

She mearde har cearke an' puddins. She say they want ter be mearde a month afore yer earte 'em, she bearke fer the family an' fer people wot keep a-poppin' in.

I say: "Tha's a rummin yew want ter mearke all o' tha' grub." She say: "Wot yew won't ter remamber is tha' tha's more blessed ter give than ter receive. Arter all, tha' is Christmas time."

Enyhow I'm startin' ter mearke a short list o' things I're hard har say she want.

Tha's no good a-gittin' wot sh're alriddy got. She want a new skatt fer the winter, but tha' could be a problem corse I dorn't know how far round she is, an' if I arsk har tha'll give the gearme away. Then I dorn't know wot colour she want, so I think I'll give the skatt a miss.

Then I hed a bit o' luck. Wen she wus a-washin' up, she wus a-mobbin' about har ole fryin' pan. She say: "The time I spend a-cleanin' this ole pan wen I might be a-doin' suffen else. Wot I want is one o' them none stick pans."

I thort: "Tha's a good idea. I'll git har one fer Christmas, in fat I'll git two, one fer Christmas an' one fer har bathday on December 20." Now tha's wot I cal gorn the second mile.

I had a look in har cupboard. She hed three skatts in there an' she cen unla wear one at a time.

My mind wus mearde up. I'll git the pans. I carn't wairt ter see har fearce wen I giv' em tew har. At least tha's suffin' she want.

I nearla fergot ter tell yer she arsked me ter write "Happy Christmas" on har cearke. I put "Happy Christmas" without the "t". I carn't tell yer wot she called me!

Happy Christmas ter yew Mr Editor an' all o' your staff. Did yer know my missus met Mr Deputy Editor Martin Kirby wen we cum up ter Norridge?

She thort he wus werry nice. She dint stop torkin' about him all the way a-cummin' humm. I carn't mearke tha' out.

An' ter all o' them people wot read me, rite ter me an' use my EDP phone line.

"Tha's a rummen yew want ter mearke all o' tha' grub."

All tha' spare wood? Tha's a bit o' a saw point wi' the missus

January, 1996

Well tha's all ova fer another year - Christmas I mean. We're had a nice time, though the missus say tha'll be a treat ter git back ter normal - wotever tha' is.

The missus was plearsed wi' har fryin' pan fer har bathday on the 20th, but a bit surprised ter git another one fer Christmas. I'd even put a bit o' pink ribbon around the handles an' wrut "Allmy love, Michael". She thort tha' wus nice.

She bort me a new bleard fer my bow-saw an' a gallon uv emulsion pairnt fer the back-plairce, so yew cen see how har mind is a-warkin'.

The missus say: "Now Christmas is ova I hope yer'e a-gorn ter git out in the shud an' do suffin'. Ye're got all o' yar tools an' all tha' wood, why dorn't yer use it up out o' the way?"

Even I thort tha' wus a good idea. I hed bin a-wonderin' wot ter do wirrit.

The I hed a brairn wairve. I'd mearke sum stair gairtes fer bungalows. I wus a-tellin' the missus about it.

She say: "Do yer think there's a call forrum?" I say: "Corse there is, every bungalow should hev one."

She say: "Bungalows dorn't hev stairs." I say: "I know tha' but tha's got nothin' ter do wirrit. I went in a blook's house not long ago an' he hed an oar a-hangin' in the hall, but he din't hev a butt."

"Look at all them people a got piarners. Tha' dorn't mean ter say they cen play 'em. Enyhow, I think I'll give it a go. I'll mearke a pattern so people cen see wot they look like, then the customers cen hev wot size they want."

The missus say: "I hope ye'rre right but I can't think they're gorn ter be as popla as all tha!" I say: " Trust yew ter pour cold water on the plan afor I even statt. The trouble wi' yew is yew hen't get ner fairth."

"Look at Ken Dodd's broken biscuit factory an' his treacle mine - they're buth dewin' everso well. Yew're just got ter think o' suffin' different."

So we set down an' hed a good chat about it an' b'the time we finished the missus agreed wi' me tha' tha' mite wark an' we'd put an advert in the EDP.

As a result things are fairly good in my household at the moment. But yew know the missus - she's like a volcano. She cen flair up at any time so tha' pay ter tearke each day as it cum.

"Every bungalow should hev one."

This here keep-fit lark mearke me tired out

February, 1996

The missus say: "Afor I married yew I wus everser fit. I played netball, tennis an' hockey, an' I did a lot o' bikin'. I biked a hundred mile in one day. Since I've stopped a-doin' tha' I fair ter be a-gorn downhill, an' tha's time I did suffin' about it afore tha's too lairte."

I dorn't know wot yew think, but I think she' gone uva the top this time. She're gone inter this here keep-fit lark. Tha's called "Miss Craig's twenny-one day shairpe-up." There's pictures uf a mawther a-doin' things wot dorn't look natural. If the missus cen dew all o' them tha'll be a miracle. Tha' tearke about half an hour ter git tru this here programme.

I tell yer wot, tha' mearke me fair tired out just a-watchin' on'er. She say tha's either gorn ter kill or cure so she's a-gorn ter stick it out.

She go' in a bit orra panic tuther night. One o' the things she hadter do wus ter lie on har back on the floor wi' har legs up like ridin' a bike upside down. She looked a job.

Enyhow, wen she finished she wus stuck fast. She say: "I carn't git up, girrus a hand."

She reckoned tha' wus a bloomin' good job I wus there corse she say: "I'd a hed ter lie there all nite." She say tha' tha' git less pairnful the more yer do it. This a bin a-gorn on fer about a fortnight now an' she say she begin ter fair tha's doin' har good. B'the time she git tru this programme she should fair as fit as a fiddle an' be more confident. So if I put a foot wrong from now on I'm forrit.

Wen she ent on the floor, she's a-sittin' on a chair, back strait, hans on har knees, eyes shut, movin' har hid from side ter side an' up an' down.

She look suffin' like a robot. I say: "Wus gorn ter happen arter twenny-one days?" She say: "I statt all uva agin. Tha' could go on rite tru the summer."

I tell yer wot, I're just about hed enuff on it. If tha's wot I're got ter put up wi' fer har ter git fit, I'd rather hev har how she wus. She dorn't want me ter tork or hev the television on corse she reckon she carn't concentrairt.

So if ever yar missus go out of an evenin' an' yewd like someone ter hev a yarn wi' just give us a ring an' I'll be uva like a shot.

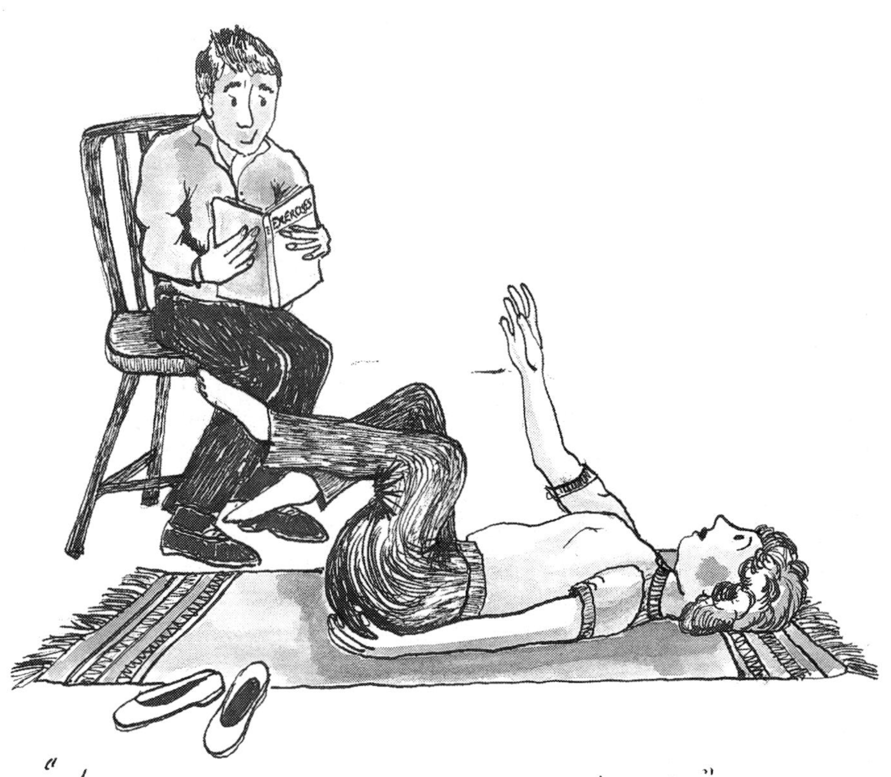

"I car'nt git up, girrus a hand."

Missus was so pleased ter see me

March, 1996

As Victor Meldrew 'ud say: "I dorn't believe it!" We all seem ter say tha' wen things go wrong. Tearke larst Sundy, we go' up like we allus do, hed our brakfust an' went ter Chapel. Oh yis, I must tell yer this. There wus a time in this here sarvice wen the preacher reckon we should pray fer ourselves fer all our sins an' all o' the things we're done wrong uva the larst week.

Tha' took a minute a two. Tha' wus long enuff fer me, tho' the missus reckon she wanted five minutes at last. I larft. I say: "Wud yer want all o' tha' time for? Wot a yer bin up to now?" She din't say nothin' but I thort all the more.

Arter dinner she wanted me ter tearke har ter se sum o' har famly. She're got eny amount on 'em. I're bin married fer fotty-tree year an' I hent met 'em all yit. I hairt wisitin'. Tha' seem ter me te be a wairst o' time, but jus' ter keep har happy I took 'er.

I stopped the car at Warcut just' ter hev a gairze at the ole sea. I say ter the missus: "Shall we hev a jam along the front." She say: "Tha's too bloomin' cold." I say: "Suit yerself, I'll go on me own." So orf I go.

Then the missus throt she'd cum an' meet me, so she go' out o' the car an' locked har door (she en't gorn ter be too plearsed wen I tell yer this). I dorn't believe it! She'd locked har ole long blue cutt in the door.

As she say, there wus two things she could a done. One, tearke har cutt orf an' freeze ter death, or two, stand where she wus an' pretend nothing' wus wrong. She thort keepin' where she wus wus the best bet.

Arter a time I cum back. I say: "Git in the car, you'll git the pip." She say: "Undo my door then I cen." I carn't ever remember har bein' ser pleased ter see me. My hart she wus suffen cold. One o' har hands wus white. I say: "Why din't yer put yer hands in yer pockets?" She say: "Hev yer ever tried ter git two hands inter one pocket?" I hatter larf but she din't hev too much ter say on account o' har fairce bein' ser cold.

She warn't airble ter open har mouth wery well. I put the car heater on an' she began ter thaw out. She say: "Le's go humm - I dorn't want ter go ner further." I thort: "Good, tha's an ill wind tha' dorn't blow someone sum good."

An' another thing, tha's my bathday today - March 1. I bet she'll fergit!

"She'd locked har ole blue cutt in the door."

Bit o' excitement over triplets

April, 1996

There bin a bit o' excitement round here lairtly. Tha' ent wery orfen we hev triplets in our willage. I're bin here all o' my life an' I're never known the likes afore. The tree boys, Bill, Ben an' George were born at Brightmere Farm next door ter me.

The triplets were tree bull carves. Jo who own an' look arter this hard o' cows told me she're bin in cows all har life an' tha's the fust time tha's ever happened on the farm afore. Jo knew the cow wus gorn ter carve, but arter she hed two onum, she thort, "Tha's it", then blow me there wus another one. Jo an' Gordon who help har ter look arter 'em are uva the mune. They luv all o' their cows but this mother is wery special right now.

Just fer the record, I must put suffen rite. In my larst letter I finished by a'sayin tha' wus my buthday on March the fust an' I bet the missus ud fergit. Well she dint...Tha' wus a tan up fer the books. She sent me a nice card wirra cricket pitcher on the front. (She know I like cricket) an' inside she wrut, "Wi luv from yar missus, you're good fer a few more runs yit". Warn't tha' good o' har ter do tha'.

She cen be like tha'. Sometimes I think she dorn't want ter know me, then the next minute she cum up wi' suffen like tha'. Ter top it all she layed on a party at nite wi' sum friends o' ours, but at the ind o' the day I think she enjoyed it more an wot I did.

She hed a few small harves an' wus in no fit stairt ter do all the washin' up. She say, "Um gorn ter bed, yew cen do the washin' up in the mornin'." I thort ter myself, "Thankyer wery much a Happy Buthday ter yew an all." Fer a present she got me a garden fork, tha' mean I're now gotta teach har how ter use it!

A lot o' yar readers hev arsked me how the missus is a gittin' on wi' har keep fit. Well she's a doin' har exercises an' she say she fair a lot stronger an' I cen prove ter yer tha's rite. Tuther mornin' we went inter the Bearkers at Stallum.

Tha' wus a cold mornin' so the door wus shut. The missus opened it an' we buth went in. She tried ter close the door agin but found tha' wus hard wark. Tha' so happened there wus a young man a tryin' ter git in. They were pushin' one aginst tuther. In the ind the missus said she wus sorry. He say, "Tha's orite, I aren't gorn ter argue wi' yew, yew must be as strong as an ox."

The mawther behind the counter say ter the young man, "Wot would yew like?" He say, "Tree cream doughnuts, - no mearke it four. I need ter build maself up in cairse I cum up aginst this woman agin."

"You must be strong as an ox."

Such hard wark tellin' 'em the rules o' cricket

May 1996

I tell yer wot, there's sum mess o' water gone under Potter Ham Bridge since I larst wrut ter yer. Tha's like this 'ere, I're bin ter America. Our mawther Carol is married ter an American so I thort tha' wus about time I went ter wisit his famly.

They live in California at Santa Maria right next ter the sea an' the sarf beaches, but do yer know I niver saw a cowboy all the time I wus there. Wen I left England tha' wus cold enuff ter freeze a brass monkey, but wen I got there tha' wus 75 ter 80.

The missus din't go. She reckon twalve hours in the air wus too much fer har an' she dorn't like it if she carn't hev the winda open. Then as she say someone a-gotta keep atome ter look arter the cat.

On the Satada mornin' they took me ter watch a bairseball gairme. Tha' looked a rummon ter see grown up men playin' a gairme wot we used ter call rounders wen I wus a boy. I told 'em I wus more inter football, but they hant iver hard o' Norwich City or Rober Chase. Cum ter tha' they'd niver hard o' Ipswich either.

Then I tried ter tell 'em about cricket. My hart tha' wus hard wark. I told 'em there are two teams wi' 11 men apiece an' one team cum out an' the other team keep in, but two o' them wot are in cum out until one o' them is out, then he go in an' another one wot wus in cum out in his plairce, til all o' them wot were in cum out ter go in agin.

Then the other team hev a go an' tha' statt all uva agin. I dorn't think they berlieved me wen I said tha' could go on fer four dairs an' in the ind nobodda win. I told 'em tha' wus a good English gairme but I dorn't think they hed a clue wot I wus a-torkin' about.

My missus reckon she cen understand them not knowin' about cricket corse she dorn't understand it either. She dorn't like cricket, niver hev done, tha's too slow fer her likin'. She go orf the deep ind about it sumtimes an' reckon I must be sorft sittin' a-watchin' tha' all day.

She say: "Tha's a bloomin' pity yew hen't got nothin' batter ter do wi' yar time." She'd rather watch Ready Steady Cook. (Not tha' tha's a-doin' a lot o' good!)

Readin' atween the lines I think the missus managed wery well on har own an' she warn't uva the moon so ter spairk wen I cum humm. A mairte o' mine who din't know I'd bin away say ter me: "Hev yew chenged yar car?" I say: "No, why?"

He say: "I dorn't know how ter say this but there a-bin a blue car in yar yard orf an' on uva the larst week an' yars is red." I aren't a bit surprised corse I know wot she's like an' so der yew.

No doubt tha'll all cum out in the wash but she hen't said nothin' about it ter me as yit.

Too much o' tha' salad fer dinner mearde me turn a shearde o' green

July, 1996

I hent felt up ter a lot this larst week a more, but the missus say: "I dorn't think yer bad enuff ter go ter the doctor. Wen we go out us mornin' we'll go inter the kamist's an git suffin' ter help yer." So we did. The missus done all the torkin'.

She say ter the blook: "Tha's my ole man, evrything he airt seem ter go ter his stummock." He way: Tha sound ter me as if he mite a got a jarm. Feed im on suffin' lite lika salads an' fruit fer a few dairs an' plenty o' lemon barley an' see how he git on."

So wen we got humm I hed a glass o' lemon barley, then the missus mearde me my fust salad fer dinner. Tha' hed evrything in it bar the kitchen sink, even sum raw carrot. I say: "Yew know I dorn't like raw carrot." She say: "Tha's good fer yer eyes." I say: "Tha's an ole wive's tairl."

She say: "Maybe, but yew never did see a rabbit a wearin' glasses." I say: "There's nothin' rong wi' mer eyes." She say: "Tha's got nothin' ter do wirrit. I know wus best, if yer want me ter look arter yer, yer airt wot I gi yer." Wi' tha' lot she mearde me drink another glass o' lemon barley.

Arter dinner the missus went up ter the Pust Orfice. She sor a mearte o' mine an' she told um I wus atum wi' my stummock an' din't fair too sharp.

"Wot he want," he say, "is hadd boiled eggs, an' suffin' else wus good is spugetty. They airt a lot o' tha' in Italy. I wus there in the war an' I know wot Um torkin' abowt. I bet Michael dorn't know an Italian wi' a bad stummock." She cum humm an' told me all o' this. I say: "Cum ter think on it I dorn't know an Italian wirra good stummock either."

Enyhow she done me sum hadd boiled eggs an' another glass o' lemon barley. Then she boiled me sum o' this here spugetty. Tha's sum rum tack ter git rid on but the missus stood uva me ter mearke sure I din't hull it away.

She hed a phone call from har friend Lily. I could hear 'em hevin' a good ole round about me. Tha' mearde me fair 10 times wass listenin' to 'em. The missus say: "Lily is a comin' round ter see yer. She say she're got suffin' ter cheer yer up."

She cum arter tea an' brort me an egg custard wi' nutmeg on the top. The missus say: "Hev sum on it now." I say: "Um full up." She say: "Tha's good o' har ter bring it, yew cen manage sum on it now, then yew cen finish it orf afore yer go ter bed."

Lily say: "He look orite." The missus say: "He en't too bad, he's just orfa his grub."

She mearde a cup o' tea fer buth o' them, but she mearde me hev another glass o' lemon barley. I tell yer wot um gorn ter fair batter termorra even if I arn't. An' suffin' else, I dorn't care if I never hev ner more lemon barley in this life nor the next.

"I dorn't care if I never hev ner more lemon barley"

Lovela dair trip ends wi' a bit o' a surproise

June ,1996

The missus say: "We dorn't seem ter see a lot o' each other now-adairs. Tha's time we did suffin' abowt it." I say: "Um happy enuff as we are, aren't yew?" She say: "Yis, but wunt tha' be nice if we cudd hev a day tergather all on our own?" I say: "I'll think o' suffin'."

Then blow me the next a mornin', thro' the pust we hed a latter from Ray Davis o' North Walsham. He organise these here train trips for NENTA Trairn Tours. Well bor tha' set har orf.

There wus dair trips gorn all uva the plearce, but she fancied the one tha' wus gorn ter Portsmuth, so she rung up an' booked a couple o' seats. The missus say: "Tha's all fixed up. We'll hev our own tairble. We leave Norrdge at seven in the mornin' an' git back at harf after leven so yew'll hev me ter yerself all day." I thort ter merself: "I cairn't wairt."

As things tarned out, tha' wus a lovela day. Unless yer want ter learve yer seat fer one reason or another yew cen sit tite the hool while, corse they bring grum an' drink round all the time. The missus injoyed tha', an' I tell yer wot, she hed har share o' small harfs.

She even let me hev one on account o' me not hevin' ter drive. Wen we got there we went acrorse ter the Isle o' Wight an' cummin' back we saw the QE2 then a-gorn inter Southhampton. She's a gret ole ship. I're never sin har afore. Then we went round the harbour an' hed a look at our Nairvy - wus left on it.

The missus wus a lookin' forward ter seein' sum sairlors but she din't see one. She wus rite upset abowt tha'. Comin' humm she say: "Tha's a pity I din't see a sairlor corse tha's one thing I wus a lookin' forward to. Where d'yer think they're all gone?"

I say: "I dorn't know, dorn't keep on abowt it." She say: "Wen I warked at the Exchange my galfrend knew a sairlor an' she used ter say he wus werry nice, tho' I hed an RAF boy." I say: "Yew did! Wen? Yew never did tell me abowt im." She say: "Yer never did arsk." I say: "Well Um arskin' yer now. Wen wus all this a gorn on?" She say: "Round abowt the time I met yew. He wus stairtioned at Honingham. I orfen think abowt im - wonderin' how he's gittin' on."

"He wus a nice boy, he took me out fer a meal in the city on his twenty-fast bathda."

I say: "How old were yew?" She say: "Nearla airteen." I say: "Yew were nearla airteen wen I met yer. Do yer mean yew were a carryin' on wi' him an' me at the searme time?" She say: "Onla a little while. I chose yew an' din't see him eny more. I orfen wonder if I mearde the rite choice, but tha's no good thinkin' abowt tha' now. Wus done is done fer batter or fer wass an' all tha'."

I say: "Thanks verry much, yer're rearla mearde my day." She say: "Dorn't gorn worra abowt tha'. Tha's a long time ago now. I still luv yew - I think!"

"We hed our own tearble."

A spot o' bother at the kissin' gairte...

August, 1996

Since the watha a got batta there seem ter be sum mess o' people about our willage. They're left their ole cars atum an' found their walkin' boots instead.

This a all cum about since a lot o' our footparths a bin opened up agin. New oak sign pusts tha' say "Public Footpath" are all uva the plairce.

Tha's luvly ter see 'em used agin at larst. Yew cen hev a nice long or a short walk wirrout a worrin' about gittin' hit birra mutta car.

They were used a lot wen I wus a boy few a short cut ter the chach or the allotments, but since we hed the bloomin' ole cars people hent felt a short cut is wath it. Now they're bein' used fer the pleasure o' gorn thro' the filds an' gittin' inter the countraside.

I took the missus on one on 'em. We went acrorse a fild to a kissin' gairte unla the gairte ent there now, but the pusts are, so yew cen see which way ter go. She say: "I remember kissin' gairtes. We useta stand agin' one o' them wen we were a cortin. Hed yew fergot tha'?"

I say: "Yew cen see there's no gairte here now." She say: "Carn't we pretend. No one cen see us, we're miles from enywhere." She allus git me flummexed wen she tork like tha'. In the ind I say: "I think we orter be movin' orf, I dorn't like the look o' tha' sky."

"P'raps yer'e rite," she say, an' we statted ter walk agin. I thort I got out o' tha' wery well an' she'd fergot about kissin' gairtes b' the time we got humm. I think tha'll pay fer me ter keep away from tha' footparth just ter be on the sairf side.

The missus may not be too plearsed wen I tell yer this, but there's a motive in all this walkin' about. She's a-puttin' on too much wairt an' she think if she walk a lot she'll lose sum on it.

She put on a pair o' trousers tuther day an' she hatter use an elastic band round the button afore she could git 'em ter dew up. She reckon there's two things she cen dew ter improve matters - one, ter lose wairte, or, two, I'll hatter git har sum new clothes. I reckon tha'll be cheaper fer har ter keep a-walkin'.

She say: "I orter be more active instead o' sittin' about of an evenin'. I orter be on a committee or suffen ter keep me busy then I wunt think about eartin' ser much." I say: "Committees are a wairst o' time. They're just a hanful o' people wot keep minutes an' wairst hours. I'd a thort yew knew tha', yer'e bin on enuff in yer time." She say: "Trust yew ter put a spanner in the warks."

"Carn't we pretend?"

My fust thorts warr 'She's gorn ter beat me up'

September,1996

Sum o' yar readers seem ter think I cum down hard on the missus.

All I cen say is tha' if yew'd summered an' wintered har as long as I hev, then yew'd know wot I mean.

Ter be fair, she hev got a few good points - at least one or two. She's good at gittin' up in the mornin'.

Orf hand I carn't think wot the tuther one is. But wi' all this nice wather tha' mearke it easier fer har ter it out o' bed. She git up fust, let the cat out, then she look out o' the winda an' give a runnin' commentry on wot she see.

Arter tha' she sing an' whistle. Um a slow statta an' I dorn't want tha' sort o' thing.

I say, "Wot the flyin' do yer want ter be ser bloomin' happy for this time o' dair?" I think tha's har way o' mearkin' sure I dorn't nod orf agin, a marster plan so ter spearke, ter git me out o' bed.

Mind yew tha's still unla harf arter six, an' there's no need ter be about tha' time o' daire, least o' wen yer'e retired. I git up tryin' ter feel good ter be alive just like har, but I find it hard wark.

Enyhow I gorn git my EDP hopin' there mite be suffin' in there ter cheer me up. Wen I cum back inter the house the missus wus on the wark top wi' the copper stick in har hand.

My fust thorts warr, "She's gorn ter beat me up or suffin'." (Well yew dew hear o' tha' sort o' thing happenin' these dairs) I could see b'the look on har fearce she ment busness.

I could handle it, but I unla hoped the pustman din't cum wi' the water bill corse he'd a bin in forrit.

She say, "Oh um suffin' glad yere back luv," or wads ter tha' effect. I say, "Wot a yew a doin' wi' the copper stick?" She say, "Um defendin' merself."

I say, "Aginst wot?" She say, "The cat a brort a rat in, tha's a foot long." I say, "If yew'd a shut the door the cat wunt a bin airble ter git in."

She say, "The door wus shut, she jumped in the winda wirrit." I say, "Where is it?" She say, "Ahind the fridge." The cat wus gorn mad. I called it "Stupid" an got wrong. I say, "Girrus a hand ter pull the fridge out ter give the cat a chance." She say, "Um not movin'. If yer carn't doit alone yew'll hatter phone the Council or dial 999." I say, "Dorn't tork ser sorft. Pull yarself tergather do. The rat'll cum out sooner or lairter then the cat'll git it. She's hevin' a good time. Tha'll give har suffin' ter do."

Arter a little while I did manage ter git the missus on the floor agin.
Then she let out a yell. She say, "Tha's out an' the cat a got it." Tha' wus
a playin' wirrit in the back yard. Tha' wus a poor little ole mouse about two
inches long.

Missus lorst har voice - a dream cum true!

October, 1996

Peace on earth an' goodwill to all men. Tha's suffin' we hear at Christmas time. Well Christmas a cum arly fer me this year. In fact Um on cloud nine.

Tha' ent nothin' ter larf about realla, but tha's all ter dew wi' the missus. A few dairs ago she hed a sore thrut. She reckon she got it wen they combined the fild o' barley, wirral the much an' dust a-flyin' about rite near our front door. I told har tha' wern't nothin' ter dew wirrat, but hold yew hard, I got a sore thrut anall. She wus suffin' plearsed I got it as well as har. She say: "Now yew know how Um a-sufferin'."

So there we were dosin' ourselves wi' boiled onions, honey an' lemon. I warn't as bad as har, an' arter a time the missus lorst har voice. Sum o' yew may say, "Poor ole Norah", but as far as Um concarned tha' wus suffin' I thort ud never happen. Ter hev har not bein' airble ter answer back wus a dream cum true. Tha' did mean I hatter keep at hum ter look arter har in cairse someone cum ter the door, or ter answer the phone. I arn't orfen there durin' the day, so wen the phone rang an I answered it, tha' just went ded.

She say (as best she could): "Who wus tha'?" I say: "They just put their phone down." So wot go on here wen Um away I leave ter yew ter wark out fer yarselves.

Cum day two she wus no batter, in fact she couldn't mearke a noise at all but we got along orite wi' har a noddin' har hid an' pointin'. She say: "Um sorry I carn't tork" (in a wispa) "but wen I git batter I'll mearke up forrit." I thort, "I bet yew will anall."

Nexta day, I began ter fair sorra forra. I say: "I think this agone far enough. You orter go an' see the doctor an' let him hev a look at yar thrut." She say: "I think fer once yew could be rite."

So I rung up the sargery forra pointment an' orf we go ter Stallum. He giv har sum red pills an' said they'd clear up the problum. I say: "How long will it be afore she cen tork agin?" He say: "Not too long." I say: "Tha' mean I batter mearke the best onnit while it larst." He larft but the missus din' look too amused.

She hatter hev four o' them pills a dair, an' wen she got up on the foth dair she reckon she begun ter fair a lot batter. She say: "If tha's wot four pills ull do, wot ull I be like b'the time I're hed twen'y? I'll be jumpin' uva the moon." So tha' look as if she's a-gittin on the mend agin.

Um rather pleased she's a-feelin' batter, but I must admit tha's bin nice bein' quiet fer a few dairs.

Praps she could arrairnge ter lose har voice agin sum time - once a year ud be about rite, once a month ud be even batter.

Missus end up in a good ol' pickle

November, 1996

Yew know yew reckon yew'd slip round an' see me an' the missus wen yew cum ter Hicklin'. Yew still can, an' we'd mearke yer wery welcome, but I'd be grairtful if yer dorn't cum just yit. Wairt a bit longer till things sattle down.

Tha's the missus, if yew understand wot I mean. She're a bin intr mearkin' jam. She're mearded two lots of plum. My hart tha' a bin a job. I kept out o' har way. I find tha's the best way ter help har. I did try once afore last year an' got suffin' rong so I larnt mer lesson.

Ter me tha' seem a simple thing ter do. Yew boil up all the fruit an' sugar, then purrit inter jars, but fer dairs artar evra cup handle yer git hold on is sticky. Yew put the pearpa on the tearble, wen yer go ter pick it up tha's stuck.

Cupboard handles an' the kittle all seem ter suffer, but the wasst of all is the lino on the backplearce floor. If yew go in there in yer socks - well at least yew aren't a-gorn ter slip on yer backside. I say ter the missus: "Why dorn't yer git yar dwile an' wash this here floor." She say: "I hent done yit. Um gorn ter mearke sum chutney next."

She cum humm wirra bag o' red bairt. She reckon tha's good stuff fer mearkin' chutney.

Wot I carn't mearke out is how cen she mearke ser much blummin' mess wen she do enything. Wi' the jam evrything wus a sticky mess but this here red bairt stuff seem ter achanged the culler o' evrything in the backplearce.

The towels, flannels, an' sink - even the soap - were a nice red sheard an' ter look at the missus' hands, yew'd think she'd got sum rare complairnt. In the ind she did mearke seven jars an' tha's wery nice though I say it merself.

The next thing ter be sacrificed wus a gret ole marra. Yew never see such a big un. Out cum Mrs Beeton yit agin. Wi' carvin' knife in har hand she cut inter this thing wi' a look o' pleasure on har fearce. I din't like the look o' tha' there knife.

Pickled onions cum arter the marra, but tha' tanned out ter be a smooth operairtion. Wass wus ter cum. A mearte o' mine from Ingham Corner brort sum hossradish roots. The missus wus suffin' plearsed wi' tha'. She screapred it, then currit up inter little bits.

Tha' wus wen she put it in the grinder tha' the trouble started. Tha' wus enuff ter blow the top o' yer hid orf.

I dorn't know wot CS gas smell like but tha' carn't be a lot wass than hossradish. Tha' mearke yer nose an' eyes run suffin' bad. Even the cat ran out o' the house ter git sum fresh air.

I say ter the missus: "Do yew think we orter eart tha?" She say: "Why not?" I say: "If tha' mearke yer nose an' eyes run like tha' wot must tha' do ter yer stummick?" She say: "Dorn't mearke ser much bloomin fuss."

"Even the kittle seemed ter suffer."

Buthday afore Christmus for missus

December, 1996

How time fly. Tha' dorn't seem a year ago wen I wus a-tellin' yew how I'd got the missus a none stick fryin' pan fer Christmus. Well, eva since then she're bin a-tellin' me wot a good thing tha' is. In fact she reckon tha's the best thing I eva did buy har, an' tha' she dorn't know how she eva managed wirrout it.

I dorn't know if yer think Um gorn ova the top ter year, but as I go round the shops I nuttice tha' not onla cen yet git none stick fryin' pans, but yer cen git saucepans, buntins an' cearktins. Did yer know tha'? So mer mind is mearde up. I'll git the set. If tha' ent gorn the second mile, I dorn't know wot is. Um sure she'll be suffin' pleased. Arter all, tha's no good a-gittin' suffin' she dorn't want.

I're got a new pair o' shoes. The missus reckoned tha's suffin' I wanted on account o' my olduns a-tearkin' in water, but the nice thing about it is the missus bort 'em for me. She reckon they'll do fer my Christmus Box, so tha's me sorted out.

I know Christmus is a few weeks orf but the missus is a-gittin' excited about it. She like Christmus, allus hev done, so at the moment she's sweetness itself. Watha tha's the lull afor the storm, or watha tha's a-leadin' up ter suffin' ramairn ter be seen.

I keep a-torkin' about Christmus, but I mustn't fergit har buthday cum a few dairs afore tha'. Tha' mean I shall hatter git har suffin', but comin' ser cluss ter the 25th is a bit too much.

If tha' could a cum the ind o' January tha' would a bin a bit more sense, but I can't do nothin' about tha' now. She're bin a-hintin' she'd like a rockin' chair.

I say, "Wot the flyin' dew yer want one o' them for?" She reckon they look nice an' hummly, an' tha' ud be luvely ter rock away if she wanted a snooze.

Arter spendin' all tha' on er fer Christmus I thort a bag o' wine gums an' a nice card ter mark the occairsion would be anuff.

But she'd got this all planned out corse the next thing she cum up with was a mearl order book wot somebody hed let har hev. She say, "Here yer are, tha's the one I'd like." I din't look at the bloomin' chair, I looked at the price onnit. I say, "I aren't a-spendin all tha' on yer."

She say, "Lissan ter me a minute, tha's the price ready mearde. Tha's half tha' DIY an' tha' include screws, glue an' cullor stearne yer want. Yer'e bin a carpenter all yer life, yew can manage ter knock tha' up."

I say, "Tha' ent as easy as all tha'. Tha' dorn't rock unless yer mearke it rock. Tha's like ridin' a bike. Wen yer stop a-pedalin', tha' stop, then yer

blunder orf." She say, "Cum on, git it for me. If yer loved me yer would."
I say, "I'll think about it." She say, "Thanks everser much luv," an' gi me
a kiss on my bald patch.

Sometimes I dorn't know wot ter do fer the best.

PS Happy Christmus ter all onya.

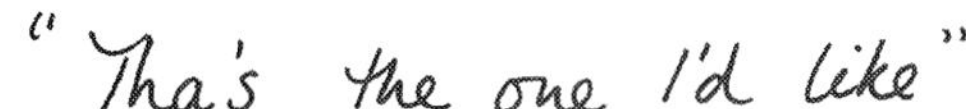

Always said the missus had got a screw loose...

January, 1997

I thort the missus managed the dairs a-leadin' up ter Christmus werry well. Evrathing wus warked out an' she wus in a good mind, that is until Christmus Eve. Of all the times ter lose the screw out o' har glasses!

There we warr, buth on us gorn about on our hands an' knees a-lookin' fer this little ole screw. She hed a magnifyin' glass. She looked like Sherlock Holmes.

In the ind we giv it up as a bad job. So if ova the holdy you see a woman about five foot airt an' grey grey hair an' a bit on the plump side gorn about wirra bit o' stickin' plaster on har glasses, lookin' like Jack Duckworth out o' Coronairtion Street, tha'l be the missus. Dorn't say nothin' corse she ont think tha's werry funny.

She wus plearsed wi' har bearkin' tins I hot har, at least she said she wus, until somebody giv har a cordless phone.

So if eny on yer ring me up, the chances on yer a-gettin' me are verry slim on account o' har hevin' har blinkin' phone wirra wherever she is. So instid o' one phone a-ringin' there's two. Yew niver hard nothin' like it.

You'd think there's a plearce car a-cummin' down the chimly, but she think tha's rather nice. We cen hev a tree-way yarn, an' the missus like ter say she's on har cordless phone an' she's a-torkin' in the backplearce, bathroom or hangin' out har linen. In fact I think tha's tannin' har inter a bit o'ra snob.

The missus hed yit more tins o'talc ter add ter har collection. She say: "Wudder people think I dew wirrall on it? I powder all I're got, wot more can I dew?"

Enyhow, Christmus is ova an' we had anice time wi' the famly, but the thing I dorn't look forward to is all the parties an' lairte nights tha' folla. They semm ter go on an' on. The missus, she's all forrit so I go along ter keep har happy an' ter keep an eye onner corse I know wot she's like wen she git excited.

We went ter one o' these here do's arter Christmus. Tha' wus at a new house in the willage an' the people wot live there inwited sum o' the locals so they could git ter know 'em. The bloke asked the missus.

I say: "How d'yew know him?" She say: "I hev a yarn wirrim now an' agin. He's everer nice. He asked me if I had a husband. I say: 'I'm afraid so.' He said I could bring yew if I wanted to."

I say: "Thanks werry much u'm sure." Tha' tanned out ter be a good nite.

The missus got harself up. I felt rite proud onner fer sum o' the time.

   There wus plenty o' grub an' drink an' the missus hed har fair share o' small harves. She reckon we'll hatter lay on a party in the New Year ter arsk sum o' these people back....I arn't lookin' forrid ter tha' but tha's wot she want so I'll hatter grin an' bear it.

   U'm happy ter wish yew Mr Editor, your staff, an' all yar readers wot git in touch wi' me all the wery best fer the New Year. Thanks fer yar support.

PS: Laurie and Gwen, (wherever yew are) please ring me.

"I powder all I've got."

Missus only hev eyes for har optician

February, 1997

"February fill the dyke, be it black or be it white." We aren't out o' the wood yit. Tha's a rum ole month, neither one thing nor tuther, but tha's nice ter think spring is on the way.

The missus, though, is still in har winter woollies buth day an' nite. I looked at har tuther nite just afore she jumped inter bed. I say: "Are yew comin' ter bed or gittin' up?"

Wot wi' bed socks an' other bits an' bobs she looked as if she wus a-gorn down ter Pallin' beach a-fishin' all nite.

Come February 14 tha's Valentine's day. Yer dorn't hear ser much about him now. When I wus little Jack Valentine wus as good a friend as Father Christmus.

I din't know it then but Mother ud git the nearbers ter knock on our door an' they'd leave an apple, orange or sweet, then they'd run away. Wen I wus older us boys ud go tru the willage a-puttin' the breeze up a-people ba tyin' two door handles tergather, knockin' on one door then runnin' orf.

Wen they tried ter open it, that ud rattle tuther door, an' neither on 'em could git out. We thort tha' was fun, but thinkin' about it now tha' warn't a werry nice thing ter do.

I ment ter tell yer last month the schule children put on a concert at Christmus. They took it ter Hicklin' House. Tha's a residential home in our willage. The missus wus part of it corse she played the keyboard.

The missus reckon this plairce is everser nice. Evraone is happy, tha's warm an' they look arter 'em well. In fact she say ter the manageress: "I shull hetter git my ole man in here."

She reckon she'd got a double room emty. The missus told har she warn't thinkin' about buth on us, she jus' meant me. She cum home a-larfin' an told me wot she'd said. I say: "I dorn't think tha's werry funny. I aren't ready er think about tha' yit."

She say: "Tha's wot yew think. Sometimes yew dew some sorft things. At least tha's nice ter know there's somewhere in our willage for yer ter go to wen the time cum an' I'd cum an' see yer about once a week or so."

Watha tha'll happen or not I dorn't know, but yew cen see how har mind is a-warkin'.

Yer know I wus a-tellin' yer how the missus lorst a screw out o' har glasses. As things tand out tha' didn't matter a lot corse she hatta hev har eyes tested an' tha' meant sum new glasses (more expense!).

Tha's a day the missus ent gorn ter fergit in a hurry. Not onla hev she got a good dentist, but she's now ova the mune about this blook wot tested har eyes. In fact she's still a-torkin' about him.

She reckon he's the best thing since sliced bread. The part she injoyed the must wus wen he got down on one knee an' arsked har ter look inter his eyes.

She thort tha' wus werry romantic an' she told'm har ole man never did git down on one knee all the years she'd known 'im.

Wen she wus a-tellin' me this she say: "Yer never even got down on one knee wen yer asked me ter marry yer. The trouble on it wus yer took me fer granted then, an' hev done ever since."

"Asked har ter look inter his eyes."

Rugby dream tha' wus a bit tryin'

March, 1977

I remamba my farther a-tellin' me a he cum humm on his ole bike learte one nite arter seein' his gal friend, wen he hatter stop corse there wus a tree acrorse the rudd.

He could see the roots o' this here tree one side o' the rudd, an' the branches on tuther side wi' this gret ole trunk stoppin' him from gittin' parst.

He put his bike on his shoulder, walked round the roots ter tuther side o' this tree, then he tanned round ter hev a larst look an' there wus nothin' there. I arsk yer, had he fell asleep an' wus it a dream?

Dreams can be wery real. Yew cen dream ye're fallin' orf a cliff or suffin' but they dew say yew wearke up afore yer hit the ground.

I dorn't know if she's a-gorn ter like me a-tellin yew this, but the missus dream, allus hev done. She wairke me up sum nites a-shoutin' an' torkin' in har sleep.

I lissen in ter see if I can larn anything. She even call out people's nairmes. Sum on 'em crop up uva an' uva agin, but never mine. I carn't mearke tha' out but wen tha' boil down tew it, tha's just a lot o' squit and dorn't mearke no sense.

Tuther nite the missus got harself inter a bit orra stairt. She wus a-kickin' an' gorn ahid all nite, then cum seven in the mornin' there wus a lump tha' wook me up. There wus the missus sittin' on the floor. She'd bludered out o' bed.

I say: "Wot a yew a-doin' out there?" She say: "I now scored a try. Didn't yew see me run clear o' the pack? Tha's the must important try I ever did score."

I say: "Cum back ter bed." All o' this wus gorn on an' she niver wook up. I carn't mearke it out corse she dorn't like rugby - dorn't even know the farst thing about it. I got out o' bed at harf arter seven an' mearde har a cup o' tea.

I say: "Mornin' my love, hev yer had a good nite?" She say: "Yis." I say: "Did yer know yew fell out o' bed?" She say: "Tha' I dint."

I say: "Yew did. Are yer orrite? Did yer hart yerself?" She say: "Not tha' I know on."

The I statted ter arsk har about this dream an' tha' all cum a-floodin' back.

She say: "Tha' was nearla full-time an' we warr a-drawin'. I got the

ball an' ran clear an' hulled maself uva the line an' I reckon tha' wus
wen I blundered out o' bed, I remember evra one wus a-cheerin' an'
sum o' the team carried me orf. I thort 'I'll git my nearme in the
pearper termorra', an' now I fair quite sad tha' din't realla happen at
all. Tha' wus just a stupid dream."

  I say: "Fer a statt yew cen dream about me." She say: "Ye're larfin'
acorse. I might a done years ago but not now. If I did tha'd ud be a
nitemare."

I reckon tha's about time I statted ter dream.

Missus bin too busy ter look arter me

April, 1997

If yer want someone ter land yer a hand, ask a man wass busy. Dorn't ask a man tha' hent got nothin' ter do, corse he ont hev time. In other wadds a willin' hos cen allus pull.

Tha's how it is wi' the missus. She never seem ter hev time fer nothin' an yit she tearke on more an' more. I aren't complearnin' ser long as she know how far she cen go.

But tha's gittin' ter the point wen she dorn't know wot she's a-doin'. She treat the house as a plearce where she just eart an' sleep, so much so tha' wen she is here we seem ter pass like ships in the nite.

She cum humme the nite afore larst wirra arm full o' pearpers. I statted ter tork. She say: "Not now, I'm busy." Then arter a while she let out a yell. She say: "My hart I're done a job. You know tha' women's meetin' at Stalham in a week or two." I say: "Yis" (but I din't really). She say: "I hatter git tree women ter read, an' I're double booked, I're got four."

She say: "Tha's gorn ter be awkward, tha' mean I shall hetter tell one on 'em I dorn't want 'em. So she got on the ole phone an spuk ter one o' these women an she told the missus not ter worry about it. She say: "I dorn't mind standin' down," so she got out o' tha' orite.

Tha' may seem a little thing but there ent a day go by wen suffen like tha' dorn't happen. She wus in the house long enuff on Sunday fer us ter hev a frank meetin' concarnin' the situeartion an she agreed tha' she hev bin a-doin' too much an' tha' she hent bin a-lookin' arter meas she should, but in about a fortnite must o' the things she's a-warkin' on should be uva an' she promised she wunt tearke on ser much agin'.

Enyhow, I must tell yer we hed a bit o' a scare tuther mornin'. Tha' wus just brearkin' day. The missus wook me up. She say: "There's somebody in the house, Listen, cen yew hear 'em?" I say: "Yis yer rite, git up an' hev a look round." She say: "Why dorn't yew?" I say: "I know wot, we'll buth onus go."

So we git out o' bed, the missus git hold o' har umbrella. She say: "Yew go fasst." I say: "Yere the one wus armed - yew should go fasst." So we tiptoed out o' the bedroom. Nothin' wus amiss in there but when we got ter the front room door we saw a lite from underneath it.

The missus say: "There's someone in there, I'm suffen scared aren't yew?" I say: "Cum ter think about it yis I am. Less think this out. The best thing fer us ter do is me ter hull open the door then yew can charge in wi' yar umbrella."

She agreed, so I flung open the door, in go the missus like a roarin' bull, an dew yer know who tha' wus? Tha' wus a blook a-readin' the arly mornin' news on the ole telewision.

I found out learter on the missus tanned it orf the nite afore wi' this ramote control thing. Someone once told me tha' a lorry gorn parst or thunder cen set it orf. I say: " P'raps tha'll larn yer ter tann it orf proper next time. She say: "Um sorra", an' gi' me a kiss.

I carn't ever remember hevin' one at tha' time o' the mornin' afore.

Missus let fearme go to har head

May, 1997

I say ter the missus: "Git yar diary out, I want yer ter block a few deartes."
She say: "Where'er we a-gorn' gallivantin' orf to now? Ennawhere nice?"
I say: "Worstead Festival, Cromer Carnival and Aylshum Show."

She say: "U'm lookin' forrad ter tha' but I shall hatta go up ter Yarmouth
an' git a new hat an' tricollearte maself up, specially since Keith Skipper
wrutt about mi in his larst book - I want ter look ma best."

I say: "People aren't gorn' ter know who yer are jus' corse yar nearme is
in a book." She say: "No, but they know yew an' they'll put two an' two
tergatha an' cum up wi' five. They'll say: 'Tha's his missus' an' if I dorn't
look nice I'll be lettin' yer down."

Enyhow, tha' wus har reason fer wantin' a new hat, an' she's gorn ter stick
tew it, so orf we go.

The missus say ter this mawther in the hat shop: "I want a straw hat
suffen like wot the Queen wear wi' a big brim, nice an' cheap corse tha's
unla gorn ter be a one orf affair."

So the missus went tru I dorn't know how many o' these hats until she
cum acrorse the wery one she wanted. Tha' were white wirra black ribbon
round it an' tha' din't corst a lot as far as hats go.

She say: "I'll tearke this one. Now I'd like two more unla different
cullers." I say: "I realle do think yer'e gorn' a bit too far. Arter all Ayshum
Show ent exactly Royal Ascot." So I say ter her this mawther: "Dew yer
sell hat ribbons?" She brort eny amount on 'em tar chose from.

Lucky fer me she wus on my side an' said a lot o' har customers dew tha'
an' tha's everser easy ter tearke one ribbon orf an' put another one on. So
the missus did wot she said.

I thort tha' wus a wise muv on my part an' I felt wery plearsed wi' muself.
I say: "Less git humm, we got ter gorn wote, remember."

Howwumever, there wus more in store for me wen we got humm. The
fasst thing the missus done wus ter go inter the bedroom. She found the
dress she thort ud go rite wi' har new hat. Whether I wanted to or not, I hatta
endure a fashion parairde. She got this here dress on.

She say: "Do the zip up will yer?" I say: "Yew cen fergit tha' dress for
a start, yer'e never gorn ter git inter tha'." She say: "I're jus' gotta git inter
it corse tha' look rite wi' ma new hat."

She did har best ter mearke it wark ter the point tha' tha' looked rite pairnful.

Then she cum up wi' a brite idea an' said she used ter hev a gardle an' if

she could git inter tha', tha' should git rid o' the lumps an' bumps. Well, ter
watch har gittin' inter this thing wus just like tryin' ter git a gallon inter a
half gallon pot.

Tha' brort tears ter ma eyes jus' watchin' 'er. Wot tha' must a bin doin'
ter har is nobody's business, but arter the best part o' sum time she'd got this
thing inter plearce an' wus ready ter try on har dress agin.

She say: "Now cen yer do the zip up?" Wirra little effort I got it done.
I say: " There yer go. Tha's done. Yer look orrite." So she put the hat on
an' walked about a bit.

She say: "I mite look orrite, but I're got another problem." I say: "Wus
that?"

She say: "I carn't breath but I reckon if I hev a terter a two less an' cut out
my mid-mornin' brearke, an' do a bit more joggin', I'll do it." I larft.

She say: "Tha's nothin' ter larf at, undo my zip." I say: "Now cen we go
an' wote?"

Mearkin' a rite ol' meal o' my puddin's

June, 1997

Well done Neil Haverson for suvivin' twenny-four year o' marital imprisonment. I're got twenny more notches on my rabbit stick than yew, an' I'm
hevin' people say ter me: "Howeva hev yer stuck it?"

There's no answer ter tha' one. All I cen say is: "Just liv a day at a time
hopin' tha' termorra mite be batter than the day afore."

Yew mite be thinkin' tha' twenny year on, yew an' the missus could be
a-livin' the life o' peace tergatha, but even tha' dorn't happen. Afore yew
know where yer are you'll hev a fresh invairsion o' granchildren, an' tha'
statt all ova agin'.

Not tha' I're got enything aginst granchildren. I love 'em but I hen't got
ner pairtience wirrem, but as grandads we cum in handa fer bearbysittin'
etc - I oon't spoil the fun for yer, yew'll find out wot I mairn.

Enyhow, tearke the missus (I think I mite a said tha' afore but nobodda
ever did) - she hev a full life. I never know where she is harf the time. I'm
not complairnin' corse I like a quiet life, but she dew tearke me fergranted.

Larst week she wus out evera day from Tewsdy ter Fridy, Cum Tewsdy
she wus up like a lark an' got harself up like a dorg's dinner. Yew never
see nothin' like it. She say ter me: "Yer'e gorn ter be atome all day aren't
yer?" I say: "Yis, I aren't gorn nowhere." She say: "Good. I're left a note
tellin' yer wot ter dew so we cen hev a nice meal wen I git humm. Cherrio."

Peace at larst! But I was kiddin' merself. I go inter the backplearce the
middle o' the mornin' ter mearke a cup o' corfee. Well bor I nearly hed a
fit. She hev said in the parst tha' she tell me things ter do an I dorn't dew
'em, so ter git ova tha' she left bits o' pearpa everywhere a-tellin' me wot
ter do. One note said: "Peel spuds an' scrairpe carrots, use this sorcepan,
dorn't fargit ter put the salt in."

Then there wus a dish wirra note: "Put chicken joints in here with onion
an' cut up clove o' garlic. Put in top oven on 175 degrees at 4.30pm." The
mearkin' o' the batter puddin' looked a bit complicairted, but I thort I'd hev
a go. I could onla do mer best. The thort o' fairlin' dorn't bear thinkin' about.

The quiet day tha' I'd looked forrad to wus tannin' inter a nitemare. I wus
up an' down all arternoon. I could see a problem. The missus hed told me
wot ter use ter mearke the batter puddin'.

In the cupboard she hed plairn an' self-rairsin flour. In my wisdom I
reckoned tha' batter puddin's should rise, so tha' hatter be self-rairsin flour.
The larst order o' the day wus ter put the puddin' in twenny minutes afore

she git humm but she din't say wot time she wus comin' humm.

I thort I'd wait till she cum through the door an' then shuv 'em in the oven. She could wait for twenny minutes.

The missus cum humm, in go the puddin's. She say: "Tha' smell whulla nice in here, U'm riddy fer ma meal."

Evrathing wus cooked an' I felt proud o' maself, but wen she looked at the puddin's she say: "Whatever happened ter them? Never mind yew did yar best luv. We'll manage wirrout 'em, but dorn't hull 'em away - they'll do ter sole yer boots."

Lotta ol' chat when gals meet up

July, 1997

Tuther mornin' I took the missus ter the Blacksmiths. Nor ter be shod. No, this Blacksmiths wus in Horsford. Tha'ss the plearce they chose fer this year's skool reunion fer ex-pupils o' the North Walsham High Skool fer Gals.

There wus about 20 odd on 'em cum an' enjoyed a fust-class meal wi good sarvice. They inwited me on account orra few on 'em wot can't drive. We all sat at one big tearble. Once they all got settin' down, then tha' statted.

Yew never hard nothin' like it. If women know ser much, why dew they arsk ser many bloomin' questions? I uvahard one woman say ter the missus: "Yer'e still wi' Michael then?" The missus say: "Yis I carn't find enything batteran wot I're got, but I still keep a-lookin'. Yew never know wus round the corner." They buth larft.

Then acrorse the tearble: "Dew eny on yer know where so-and-so is, an' wot about such-and-such, is she still livin' in Leeds?" an' so on. I din't know who they werra talkin' about but the missus did an' she seemed ter be enjoyin' 'erself.

There wus the stories o' their dairs at skool like chattin' up the boys from the grammar skool. I thort if I kept a-lisnin I mite larn a thing a two. Instead I hard a lot about the gorns-on in the trairn from Walsum ter Stallum.

One on 'em say ter the missus: "Do yew remember John Harris, Norah?" The missus say: "I think so." They all larft an' said: "She think so! Cum on Norah, can't yew remember him puttin' yew up on the luggage rack?"

I looked at the missus. Har fearce wus a bit on the pink side. I say tew'er: "Who wus this John Harris?" She say: "He wus a grammar skool boy all the gals like."

There wus a latter from one on 'em who warn't airble ter cum on account o' har hevin' ter go forra check-up.

They say ter the missus: "How orfen dew yew go fer yar MOT?" The missus say: "I dorn't go at all, I fair wery well an' I say, 'If it ent brook, dorn't mend it'."

Wen we got humm the missus say: "All o' them gals seem ter go an' see their doctor once a year, dew yar think we orta go?"

I say: "If tha's wot yer want then yis we'll go." She say: "I tell yer wot. Yew go fasst an' see wot he dew ter yer then if yer think tha's orrite I'll go." So she booked me in.

As I wus gorn she say: "Dorn't fergit ter tellim yer hard o' hearin'."

Tha' all went well an' he told me I wus orrite. Afor I left the doctor say: "Is there anything yer want ter tell me about yerself?"

"Well," I say, "The missus reckon Um hard o' hearin' in mer left lug." So he had a good ol' look. He say: "There's nuthin' wrong, tha's yer airge." I cum humm an' told the missus. I say: "Tha's a rummon him a-sayin' tha'. Ma rite lug is orrite an' tha's the searme airge as ma left."

All I know is, wen I read the obituaries in the EDP of a mornin' an' my nearme is missin' then I must still be alive, an 'Um grairtful.

Michael misses the missus

August, 1997

Once upon a time, years afor the dairs o' watha forecasts, farmers an' the likes ud look ter the skies fer guidance. They knew all about red skies at nite an' mornins. The sairme went fer the wind. If tha' wus in the North, tha' wus gorn ter be cold, if in the East, bloomin' cold, an' Hickling bein' a few salt breezes away from the sea, I know wot U'm a torkin' about. Once the wind git out there in the winter tha' go on fer weeks an' weeks.

The mune played it's part too - Near the burra far the storm, far the burra near the storm, not fergitten' them ole sun dorgs. So the farmers ud plan their wark b'these signs.

Tha' ole mune a got a lot ter answer for. If there's a full mine an' a North wind we git high Spring Tides an' tha's allus a worryin' time round here.

Farmers believed too tha' sowin' seeds durin' a waxin' mune gav batta garminairtion than a wainin' mune. Tha' mite still apply now, I dorn't know corse I aren't a farmer.

The mune play tricks wi' people too, in fact I're bin a mearkin' a study o' the missus ove the larst few months an' tha' seem ter me tha' cum a new mune up ter a full mune she realla is wath livin' with. She's sweetness itself an' I carn't put a foot wrong an' tha' mearke me think she luv me - well, just a little bit - but the larst harf o' the mune she seem ter tann inter diffrent passon like someone from another planet.

At this moment o' time U'm hevin' the time o' ma life. The missus a gone ter the Peak District wi' our mawther Carol an' har two gals, so I're got one week o' doin' wot I like wi' no sharp tongue arskin' me the wot, why an' wen questions; gorn ter bed an' gittin' up wen I like, watchin' cricket wirrout hevin' ter explairn about silly mid on an' orf. (She dorn't like cricket).

Yis, I took the missus ter Swaffham ter meet our Carol. On the way humm I had a good lunch at Sutton Stairth Hotel. Next dair I went ter Cromer ter see my ole mearte Keith Skipper an' had a Fish an' Chip lunch at Mara Jairne's in Garden Street; on the Wensda I cairme up ter Norridge ter Prospect House an' met one a two people I're bin wantin' ter see for a long time. I finished orf ba hevin' a nice lunch there, so all in all I han't had ter dew a lot o' cookin' or washin' up.

Arter a time I thort the hand bairson in the bathroom looked a bit datty. Tha's a rummin'. I hen't ever sin tha' afor. Then I fergot ter pay the milkman an' ter put the black bags out fer the ductcart.

The cat ran out o' grub, I ran out o' bread, the water cummin' out o' the hot tap wus cold an' the plants in the hangin' barskets statted ter kell uva so I thort ter maself, "She must abin doin' all them sort o' things."

Dew yer think U'm beginnin' ter miss har? Did I hear yew say "Yis?" Dew yer know, I think yew could be rite.

Hurry up an' cum humm luv; all is fergiven!!

A tickin' orff arter cleanin' windas

September, 1997

Arter them long hot dairs, the missus reckon she's gorter hev a sabbatical. I say: "Dew yer know wot tha' mearn?"

She say: "Cors I dew, tha's a time o' rest."

I say: " Wot the flyin' a got inter yew? All the years I warked I din't hev a lot o' rest. Yet must remamba I warked a forty-nine an' a harf hour weark wi' one weark's holdy, an' if Christmus Dair fell on a Sunda tha' wus too bad. Even Good Frida warn't a holdy till lairter on.

She say: "Then wus then an' now is now. People hev a lot more pressure now than wen we were young."

Enyhow she say: "I're mearde up my mind U'm gorn ter hev a month orf whaher yew like it or nut. Tha' should be long enuff ter git charged up. U'll still cook an' keep the house harf clean, so the next four wearks yew'll hetta git orf yar backside an' dew a bit more like the garden an' cleanin' windas, an' torkin' about windas, tha's suffen tha' want dewin' rite away so git on wirrit."

Fer once I din't know wot ter say, an' tha's sayin' suffen'. She seem ter think just a corse I're retired she should retire anall, otherwise har life is no diffrent. Thinkin' about it I spus she mite a got a point but I dorn't need all o' this. I're got enuff ter do wirrout a doin' harf har wark.

Now she's in tha' sort o' mood, there's nothin' one cen do about it as I're proved many a time uva the years.

So the next a mornin' I thort I mite as well please as tease. I got inter cleanin' har bloomin' windas. I're got all o' the gear. Wi this here thing like a windascreen wiper on yer car an a clean bit o' ole towel I soon hossed round them. I thort I'd done a good job an' she'd be suffen' plearsed but hold yew hard, she say: "Did yer say yew'd done the windas?"

I say: "Yis."

She say: "They look a job, wot ever hev yer done? They look wass now than wot they warr afore yer statted. Ent tha' a rummon, a simple little job like cleanin' a winda - carn't yew do nothin' proper? I sometimes wonder how on earth I got mixed up wi' yew. Pull yerself tergather for goodness' searke."

Arter a tellin' orf like tha' I felt about tree foot tall. I said I wus sorry but tha' wus like water orf a duck's back, so I say: "Wot I want is a wash latha." She say: "If tha's yar excuse I'll soon sort it out, I'll go ter the shop next door ter git one."

This blook in the shop din't hev a wash latha but he told har he'd got suffen' just as good, if not batta. So he showed har this here magic clorth.

He reckoned tha's wot he use. Tha's ever ser easy, a child o' five cen manage it.

   The missus larft. She say: "I'll tearke it. That should be orite fer my old man." Ha, ha.

   PS - The missus say: "Will yer tell Audrey tha' she found the tin o' mackrell in the wardrobe!"

Missus mearke a fuss ova har back

October, 1997

All I ask is fer the missus ter tell me the truth. I aren't gorn ter say she dorn't, but there are times wen she hev me on.

Tearke larst weekend, we went away, but afore we went the missus went round the house a-pullin' out all the plugs in cairse we got a storm.

Tha's wen she reckon she pulled suffin' in har back. She din't say too much about it, not enuff ter spoil the weekend, but come Mondy, known as wash day, she put on a good performance an' said har back wus wery bad an she warn't airble ter pick things orf the floor or do enything tha' wus ter cause an extra strairn.

Wot would yew a said if I'd told har ter pull harself tergather an' tha' wus nothin' ter worry about? She said I wus hard an' hant got ner feelin' an' snapped like a little ole dorg.

I knew orrite wot she wus on. She wanted me ter fair sorry for 'er. Then I thort, "Tha's onla Mondy an' I dorn't want this ter go on rite thro' the week." So I asked har wot she'd bin wantin' ter hear. I say: "Is there anythin' I cen do ter help?"

She say: " Tha's kind on yer, yew can help me ter hang mer linen out."

U'm suffen' glad mer linen line ent sin from the rood corse I felt a rite twit. She could peg 'em on the line but gitten' out o' the line basket wus a problem. So there I wus a handin' har har smalls one ba one.

She rubbed all sorts o' stuff on har back - all on 'em said they'd mearke har fair batta, but she han't got a lot o' fairth in wot she read on the packets etc.

Tha's just the sairme wen she go shoppin'. She read wot tha' say on a tin or suffen' an' if she dorn't like wot she read she wunt touch it wirra barge pole. Enyhow I wus a-lookin' in the freezer cabinet.

She say: "Wot a yew a lookin' for?" I say: "I wus lookin' at them there beefbargers."

So she picked up a packet an' hed a good ole read.

She say: "Hev yer sin wus in 'em?" I say: "No."

She say: "If tha's wot yer want yew git 'em but I wunt eart one o' 'em if yew paird me." I say: "I think I'll hev 'em. They'll mearke a good supper ternight."

She say: "Go on then but dorn't blearme me if yer keel ova."

So about nine, I cooked two o' these beefbargers an' took 'em inter the front room. She say: "They smell suffin' nice." Then I statted ter eart 'em. She stood up an' cum ova ter me.

She say: "Yer look as if yer enoyin' them. Cen I hev a tearst?" I say: "Dew yew think yew ort to?"

She say: "Yew still fair orrite dorn't yer?" I say: "Um fine." She say: "I think I'll go an' cook the other two an hev 'em."

There are times wen I carn't mearke ins ner middles out on 'er!

When I lorst the missus
on the escalairtor

November, 1997

The missus wanted ter go shoppin'. "The onla plearce I cen git wot I want is in one o' them big shops in the city." I say: "Yer know I dorn't like a-drivin' in Norridge, carn't we go somewhere else?" She say: "No. If yew dorn't tearke mi I'll git someone else ter run me up there." Tha's har way o' gittin round me. So I thort I batter mearke the effort.

Well I got there orrite - din't hit nothin', but I did go the wrong way round the car park. We found the shop. Tha' wus a grat ole plearce an' they hed sum bewaful stuff in there. She was a-lookin' fer the floor wot sold gal's dresses. She wanted one for our Lucy. We hatter go on one o' them escalairtors - bloomin' good things they are, batteran a walkin' up stairs. She soon got wot she wanted. I say: "Tha' din't tearke long, less git out o' this an' go humm." She say: "Tense a likely. I aren't gorn yit, we hent bin here five minutes. I got on fasst. Wen I got ter the bottom I looked round an' there wus the missus still at the top. I say: "Cum on, wot are yer doin' up there?" She say: "I carn't git on. Yew'll hatter cum up an' girrus a hand." So I go up agin. Wen I git there she weren't nowhere ter b'sin. I thort jus fer a minute she mite a dun a bunk. She hev said now an' agin tha's wot she mite do, but then I thort she wunt go like tha' corse she hed the house an' car keys in har handbag.

So if she din't cum down, she must a gone up. I go up ter the next floor an' a young mawther say ter me: "Can I help yer?" I looked round an' there wus dummies dressed in things I'd never sin the likes afore. I say: "I dorn't think so, my missus is parst a-wearin' stuff like this." She say: "Never, we sell a lot o' these ter the more older woman. They say tha' help ter put a spark back inter their lives." I say: "Not my missus; if yew knew har like I do yew'd know she en't short o'ra few sparks. Besides tha' ent wot I cum here for. If yer must know, I're lorst har." I wus suffen glad ter git orf tha' there floor. I felt a rite twit.

I still din't find the missus, so I went down ter the ground floor an' hed a look round an' there she wa a-tryin' on shoes. I say: "I're been a-lookin' high an' low fer yew. Where the flyin' heya bin an' howd yer git down ?" She say: "A man at the top got hold o' my arm an' helped me. He wus everser nice. He arsked me if I wus on ma own. I wus tempted ter say Yis but I thort yew'd tan up sooner or lairter." I say: "Din't yer think fer one minute tha' I mite be worryin' about yer?" She say: "No not really, I wus enjoyin' merself, I just din't think." I say: "Tha's your trouble. Yer dorn't think."

"Cum on wot are yer doin' up there?"

Dishclorths an' dusters mairke nice gifts

December, 1997

Well tha's December now an' we're on the larst lap o' the rairce leadin' up ter Christmas. The missus was a-sayin' unla this mornin': "Where eva hev the time gone? Tha' dorn't seem unla five minutes since larst Christmas. Tha's rite wot they say tha' the older yer git the quicker the time go."

She seem ter be in har normal flap, in other wads she ent nowhere near riddy, whereas me, I're got things under control. I think I're warked it well.

Wen yer think about it, I git a double dose of it wi' the missus's barthday comin' on December 20, but I hen't left it till the larst minute - oh no, I're bin a-buildin' up a list o' things I're hard har say she want. Arter all, as I see it tha's little or no good a-gittin' things she dorn't need. I lairve tha' ter other people - like talc fer the bathroom, tha's suffen she never buy an' yit she allus hev more onitt than wot she want. She say: "Wudda people think I do wirrut all? Yer powder all yer got but wen yer git on a bit yer hen't got a lot."

Then there's clothes. She fair ter me ter hev plenty o' shatts an' skatts an' things ter keep har nice an' warm, an' she's well shod. She're got two pairs o' shoes an' sum rubber boots, an' yer can' unla wear one pair o' them at a time. So fer December 20 I shall be gittin' things tha' a useful like har non-stick fryin' pan tha' I got har larst year. There's one thing I know she want an' tha's a new handle on har hoe. She ran the barra uva har other one an' brook it, an' ter hev a hoe wi' no handle is like hevin' a water tank wirra hole in it. Tha's good fer nothin' an' she must hev har hoe so she cen do har garden.

Suffen else she want is sum new dusters, sum o' them nice yaller ones. I thort if she had them tha' mite git har inter usin' one on'em an' tha' ud keep the house a bit cleaner. Well at least tha's wath a try, an' I know she badly want sum new dishclorths.

So wi' these three things plus a nice card I think I're done har werry well an' I dorn't think she'll hev eny rite ter complairn. But she like Christmas an' tha' bein' a spacial day, I're left the best till larst an' realla gone ter town this year.

From the back door ter the rudd is about 40-50 feet o' gravel an' the missus reckon tha' hatt har feet. She dorn't know yit but wot U'm gorn ter do is git har sum o' them conrairte slabs fer har ter walk on. I thort I'd git 10 on 'em this Christmas. Tha' ud git har harf way acrorse then I'll git the other 10 or so fer next year. I're ordered 'em from Stallum an' the blook is gorn ter bring 'em in time fer me ter lay 'em down afor the big day. I carn't wairt ter see har walkin' on 'em fer the fasst time. She'll be as plairsed as a dorg wi' two tairls.

We hen't mearde up our minds where ter go yit. Fer my part I dorn't mind
ser long as I cen stay atome, but at the ind o' the day I shell hatta do as U'm told.

I'd like ter wish all o' them people wot rite ter me an' phone me a happy
Christmas. Tha's good ter hear from yer an' U'm plearsed yer enjoy
reardin' mer latters. An' ter yew Mr Editor an' yar staff at Prospect House,
best wishes. Keep yew a-troshin'!

PS: As yew see, the missus hen't said a lot in this letter. Tha' mearke a
chenge. She reckon she're got a lot on har mind an' she can't think proper!

"Sum o' them nice yaller ones"

Just watchin' the washin' go round

January, 1998

Soon arter I rutt ter yer larst month we lorst a good ole friend. He'd bin in the house fer I do. 't know how many a year an' he'd sarved us werry well in tha' time. The missus knew 'im batter an me corse she had more to wirrum. But wen the ind cum the missus reckon she'd bin expectin' it on account o' him a-bein' out o' sorts fer the larst few months.

We asked the exparts who knew 'im well ter hev a look at 'im an' they said the time hed cum ter git rid on'im, corse they reckon that ud corst more ter mearke 'im batter than wot he wus wath. So me an' the missus carried 'im out o' the back door fer the larst time. As we did so I looked at har an' she hed a tear a-runnin' down har fearce. As we laid 'im ter rest under the Russian vine.

Never agin will yer hear me a-talkin' about our ole wash boiler. Tha's gone fer good this time. Mondys will never be the searme agin. We buth on us felt quite sad, but as the missus say: "Times chenge an' we hetter muv on."

There's no doubt about it I shall miss seein' water a-runnin' down the walls o' the back plearce. Most orrall I'll miss seein' the missus wi' har rid fearce an' hearin' the hulla she mearke wen things dorn't go rite.

We spent the rest o' the dair torkin' about it. Did this mean we'd hetter git the dreaded washin' machine? We go up ter Stallum ter the shop wot sold these bloomin' things an' we were shown the model tha' would be rite fer our needs.

We said we'd hev it an' they'd bring it the next a-mornin'. Afor we left the shop I asked how much they'd gimme fer our ole boiler. They larft but din't say nothin'.

The missus cum up wi' the arnser. We'd keep it in the shud an' use it ter keep tairters in. Doin' tha', she say, we woont fergit it, a nice reminder so ter speark o' the good times.

Next a-mornin' the missus wus up like a lark an' wus gorn mad in the back plearce hullin' out this an' tha' an' mearkin' room fer this new toy. Once in plearce, the missus wus excited an' soon fergot about har ole boiler an' spent the rest o' the dair a-readin' the instruction all riddy fer the trial run the next a-mornin'.

She put har linen in an' then pulled up a kitchen stool so she could watch wot wus gorn on. We were both glued tew it lookin' at the glass door like watchin' Emmerdairle Farm.

She say: "There go your shat."

I say: "Wus tha' red thing?"

She say: "Thass my skat."

I say: "I din't know yew hed a red skat."

She say: "Tha' prove yer dorn't look at me much these dairs."

There's suffen else ter cum out o' this, an' thass har copper stick. She ont want tha' enymore, so if there's enyone want it we'd let it go ter a good humm.

I hope yew hed a good Christmas. We hed a nice time wi' the famly, an' the missus wus pleased wi' all har bits an' pieces an' wus ova the moon wi' har new hoe handle, an' is a-lookin' forrid ter usin' it cum the spring. She say she dorn't want big presents or things tha' corst a lot. She like simple things in life - like me. She say sum cuttin' things sumtimes.

She say she's gorn ter mearke a few New Year's resolutions, but she ent gorn ter tell me or no one else wot they are just in cairse she brairke 'em, then nobody'll know they're bin brook.

A Happy New Year ter yew Mr Editor an' them wot help yer at Prospect House, an' all o' them wot keep a-readin' wot I rite in yer pearpa. Keep yew a-doin'!

Dentist put a smile on har fearce

February, 1998

I fair tha's about time I stood up ter mer 5ft 81/2 or (5ft 9 on a good dair) an' took drastic action.

Tha's no good, I can't go on like this much longer. Suffin' a gotter be done.

They say if yer got a problem yew should set down an' tork about it. Well I're tried tha' till U'm blue in the fearce. Tha' jus' roll orf the missus like water orf a duck's back.

Yer see in the summer time wen tha's nice an' warm, the missus is up an' about like a lark, but I wish yew could be a fly on the wall an' see wot she's like these cold dark mornins. She cum up wi' all sorts o' excuses not ter git out o' bed.

Tha's gittin' ser bad tha' b' the time she're washed up the breadkfust dishes she's peelin' spuds fer dinner. I told har how she's wairstin' ser much time wen she could be up an' dewin' suffin useful.

She blearmed me, so bein' the sort o' blook I am I said I'd git up fust at our normal time. I dorn't think I cen be fairer than tha'.

So wot Um dewin' is gittin' out o' bed, tannin' the lite on an' switchin' on Radio Norfolk. Wen she hear tha' she start ter cum to. I git the EDP an' tearke it tewer. Tha' mearke har sit up, then I let the cat in the bedroom. She jump on har bed an' statt a-lickin' har fearce as if ter say, "Wen are yew a-gorn ter git up?"

The long an' the short on it is tha' my master plan is warkin' but these things dorn't dew enuff ter git har feet on the boards. The larst part o' the plan seem ter be dewin' the trick.....

Arter all these years o' marital imprisonment I're found a way o' mairkin' the missus happy. I tearke har a cup o' tea, a dish o' porridge wirra spoonful o' honey in it an' a round o' tust wi' ruff cut marmalairde.

B'the time she're hed tha' lot, she's 95 per cent awairke an' she git out o' bed wi' little or no effort. If I can keep this pearce up, I feel U'm dewin' a bloomin' good job.

Yew remamber me a-tellin' onyer about har optishun who opened har eyes larst year, she thort he wus ever such a nice man an' din't stop torkin' about him fer months.

Well a the moment he dorn't stand a chance corse the missus a got a new man in har life an' is ova the moon. This time tha's har dentist.

She met this new blook tuther mornin'. I went wirra an' wearted fer har ter cum out. She wus gone the best part o' sum time but wen she cum ter meet me she had smile on har fearce an' said wot a lovely man he wus an' is lookin' forrid ter gorn' back agin - an' there aren't many people say tha'.

Ter be told arter the X-ray tha' she hed good bone structure really did cheer har up. Wen she go trew the willage now people say: "Hello Norah, how are yew?" She say: "U'm fine - I're got good bone structure."

The Missus and me at our Silver Wedding
I carn't see nothin' ter larf at! (Photo: D Greenacre)

If me or the car dorn't wark, missus'll fix it

February, 1998

Tha' mearke yer wunda wus gorn ter happen next! The missus reckon she's gorn ter be more assartive an' tearke control o' har life. She's thinkin' o' gittin' books an' studyin' about things tha' could help me, the family an' others.

One thing she thinks is important is ter know how a motor car wark, corse she say I dorn't. I say: "I cen statt it an' drive it. Wot else is there ter know?"

She say: "Wen tha' dorn't go, why dew yer open the bonnet?" I say: "Tha's wot yew hev ter do jus ter hev a look."

She say: "Look at wot?" I say: "I dorn't know, dorn't keep arskin' ser many questions."

She say: "Wot about if one mornin' tha' really dorn't statt, yew wunt know wot ter dew would yer? Be fair, tell the truth."

I say: "Orrite yew win agin'." She say: "I dorn't want ter know how ter chenge a gearbox or clutch, jus' the simple things, like chengin' the oil an' fittin' a new filter. All I need is a good set o' spanners an' I'll be set up. Dorn't yer think tha' mearke sense? Oh, an' I'll want two o' them things wot yer run the car on so I cen git underneath otherwise I'll git stuck."

I say: "Dorn't yer think yer tearkin' on more an yew cen chew?" She say: "No, I'm jolly sure I cen dew it. Tha's a matter o' common sense. I know yew think I'm sorft but I aren't realla. Yew ort ter know tha' ba now, so wot about it? Are yew gearme? Think o' the money you'll searve."

The money-searvin' bit won me uva so in the ind I say: "I arn't happy about it but if yew know wot yer a-dewin' on I'll let yer hev a go." She say: "Thanks luv" an' give me a nice smile. She say: "Good." The next time we go ter the libry I'll git the manual fer a Ford Fiesta 1.1 an' read all about it, dorn't worry, you'll be proud o' me in the ind dew yew see. You git the stuff an' I'll dew the job."

As if tha' weren't enuff ter swalla, the next idea she cum up with just put shivers down ma spine. She's gorn ter study Fast Aird. She say: "Hev yer thort how handy tha' ud be? Jus' suppus we were drivin' along an' saw a car in a ditch or hit a tree or suffin' an' the driver wus trapped an' there wus no one else about. There are things yew cen dew tha' could help until the plearce cum ter the rescue. Tha's jus' knowin' about such things an' yew could searve a life. Dorn't yew think tha's wath while? Dew yew really know how ter give anyone the kiss o' life?"

I say: "I're niver hed ter to do it." She say: "Tha's wot I say, unless yew know yew could dew more harm than good, but jus' ter know about the simple things tha' cen happen round the house would be handy. Yew could git suffin' in yer eye, blunder out o' bed or git a crack o' the skull on the linen prop. If I know how ter treat such mishaps, tha' ud searve yew gorn ter the doctor's."

"So wen I git the book, I'll tearke it a stearge at a time. We're got plenty o' bandages, slings an' sairfty pins. Yew can be my pairtient. I think tha' ud be nice dorn't yew, an' yew niver know, yew could git ter enjoy it!" She larft At the moment I fair wery well but fer how much longer I arsk?

Our mawther Carol singing at Bury St Edmunds

That was a party political book by Michael Brindid MPG Member of the Press Gang), on behalf of the Norfolk Party!

Michael, a Norfolk man through and through, is one of the promoters of the County's heritage, culture and dialect so generously supported by the Eastern Daily Press as well as many proud Norfolk folk the world over.

When I first got a call from him inviting me to produce "I Din't say Nothin'" I was a little uncertain about what to expect. True, I know about printing and books, and I speak the language but I was not certain how to get to Hickling or what sort of chap I was going to meet when I got there.

I need not have been so apprehensive. He greeted me with the comment that he could not believe a Norfolk man could not find Hickling and I said that I wasn't sure that anyone would want to anyway and we took it from there.

Our wives seemed to get on very well from the start, perhaps they see themselves as having something in common!

As well as being easy to work with Michael has introduced me to the delights of Hickling village, the Broad, the building trade and the Methodist Chapel. In addition to this I have discovered the excellence of Nora's Cheese Scones. In fact a certain person often enquires if I have eaten in the days leading up to business meetings (no name - no pack drill).

This is the second book I have produced for Michael. He tells me that this is the last, then again he said that about the first book. So I am sure there are more to come.

I still take the wrong turning into Hickling. Thar missus she say: "Yer gorn wrong agin." Funny how they always know!

Jim Baldwin